MEMOR
THE WESTERN
FRONT

PLACES OF REMEMBRANCE

MARCUS VAN DER MEULEN

AMBERLEY

The Gate
of
Eternal Memories

An illustration from the booklet *Menin Gate at Midnight (or The Ghosts of Menin Gate): The Story of Captain Will Longstaff's Great Allegorical Painting*, published by The Australian War Memorial, Canberra, 1929.

First published 2018

Amberley Publishing
The Hill, Stroud
Gloucestershire, GL5 4EP

www.amberley-books.com

British Library Cataloguing in Publication Data.
A catalogue record for this book is available from the British Library.

ISBN 978 1 4456 7839 9 (print)
ISBN 978 1 4456 7840 5 (ebook)

Typeset in 10pt on 14pt Sabon.
Origination by Amberley Publishing.
Printed in the UK.

CONTENTS

INTRODUCTION

Capelle Beaudignies Road Cemetery, northern France, established by the 3rd Division in October 1918.

Hargicourt Communal Cemetery Extension, France.

On 4 August 1914 the Imperial German army crossed the Belgian border and invaded the kingdom. Belgium had refused free passage for the Imperial troops and wished to retain its neutrality, a neutrality that was safeguarded by Britain. Brave little Belgium proved to be more resilient than expected. Frustrated by this resistance, German troops shot civilians, even priests, in towns such as Dinant and Leuven, where the invaders burned the medieval city centre including the centuries-old university library. Outraged by these atrocities, many British students voluntarily joined the Forces. Summer 1914 had suddenly turned into an antagonistic encounter. The Battle of the Frontiers, the Great Retreat and the Race to the Sea: Imperial Germany continued to advance until, in November 1914, the offensive was halted in the fields of Flanders and northern France. Four long years of trench warfare were to begin on what would become known as the Western Front. This would be a war unlike any other the world had ever witnessed before, a war that became known in many countries and languages as the Great War, la Grande Guerre, de Grote Oorlog. Farmers in Flanders still find bombs dating back to the years of the

First World War on a regular basis when ploughing their lands, almost 100 years after the Armistice was signed in a railroad carriage outside Compiègne. This is a war that is still remembered, vivid not only in people's minds but in the memorials that can be found near every battlefield. From the impressive arch of Thiepval to the Cross of Sacrifice in Bellenglise, the First World War has forever changed a bucolic landscape into fields of grief.

The first memorials were already being erected during the years of the war. Often these were preliminary structures such as wooden crosses marking the locations of war graves or events. After the war, the need for commemorating those who gave their lives with more appropriate memorials instigated the building of monuments and cemeteries. Some of these were private memorials, initiatives of individuals as personal monuments of grief. Others were built by national bodies such as the Imperial War Graves Commission. The design of these memorials stood in a long tradition, even if the building of memorials to the fallen was a relatively new phenomenon. Obelisks had been popular monuments for some time, neoclassical arches had been used to celebrate military successes for centuries and the memorial

Pozières Memorial and Cemetery, designed by William Cowlishaw, was unveiled in August 1930.

Headstones near Thiepval.

plaque can even be traced back to the steles erected in ancient Greece. Eminent architects were called upon to design memorials fitting their function, of which Sir Edwin Lutyens is probably the most illustrious today. His Thiepval Memorial to the Missing of the Somme has become an iconic place of remembrance and location for several official commemorations. In 2016 the memorial was the site for a centennial service attended by HRH the Prince of Wales, HRH the Duke of Cambridge, the French President and many others to honour those who were killed in the Battle of the Somme. Lutyens's design is an enormous arch that connects the past to the present and a humbling site demanding observation. The Cross of Sacrifice, designed by Sir Reginald Blomfield, has become an archetype for the British war memorial and many versions can be found throughout the world. In more recent years the notion of a memorial has broadened and shifted away from the neoclassical. The Lochnagar Crater at Ovillers-la-Boisselle, a remnant of an early explosion at the start of the Battle of the Somme, is today among the most visited memorials commemorating the First World War. And outside Langemark, Belgium, the Welsh Memorial unveiled by the Welsh First Minister and the Flemish Minister-President in 2014 consists of several dolmens surmounted by a fierce red dragon. The appearance of war memorials has changed over time. Today the Western Front is a landscape of memorials, an itinerary of monuments, parks and cemeteries, dedicated to remembering the events and the casualties of the First World War.

Above: 'This Tower is Dedicated to the Glory of God in grateful memory of the Officers, Non-Commissioned Officers and Men of the 36th (Ulster) Division and of the Sons of Ulster in other forces who laid down their lives in the Great War, and of all their Comrades-In-Arms who, by Divine Grace, were spared to testify to their glorious deeds.' The Ulster Tower Memorial near Thiepval.

Left: Mourning figure, Canadian National Memorial, Vimy.

Monuments of Grief

Loss and Remembrance

The Ypres Salient and the Battle of the Somme have become part of our collective memory. What had started in summer 1914 as a sudden war became an enduring loss. The German Schlieffen plan to invade and rapidly defeat France had failed. Belgian troops proved to be more resilient than expected, retaining a small piece

Ramicourt British Cemetery near Saint-Quentin, France, designed by William Cowlishaw. The cemetery was established days after the capture of Ramicourt by three battalions of the Sherwood Foresters on 3 October 1918.

of the kingdom on the river Yser. The United Kingdom, which had secured Belgian neutrality and its independence, was able to mobilize and cross the Channel. At the first Battle of the Marne, British and French troops were able to push back the German advance. During autumn 1914 a front line developed from Nieuwpoort on the North Sea along historic cities and towns towards the rivers Somme and Aisne. For years attempts to bring back a war of movement, by using chemical weapons or aerial warfare, did not succeed. A spring offensive in 1918 was a final attempt by the Imperial German Army to change forever the course of the war. Later that year the war finally came to an end. The Armistice was signed in Compiègne on 11 November, a date engraved in our souls as Remembrance Day. During the four long years much had changed. With more than 3,258,000 killed on the Western Front during the years of the First World War, the war became known as the Great War. A costly war with severe losses in every family, the need for memorials as a visualization of this loss – monuments to express grief – was obvious. Private initiatives resulted in commemorative crosses and modest memorial chapels. People organized themselves in societies. During the war the Imperial War Graves Commission, today the Commonwealth War Graves Commission, was established and after the war several other initiatives were founded, the Ypres League being a fine example, to commemorate those who had given their lives.

The Cross of Sacrifice, Coppice Cemetery, Haspres, France.

In the decades preceding the First World War the victory monument had developed into a war memorial. This was a transformation marking an important alteration, from celebrating a joyful occasion to the mourning of a loss. For centuries wars and battles had been commemorated by the erection of monuments to celebrate a triumph. Many of these monuments were positioned not in the setting of the victorious combat, a remarkable exception being the lion at Waterloo, but in prominent locations in towns and cities. Monuments of war had been tributes to victory. A classic kind of victory monument is the arch. Dating back to ancient times, several Roman emperors had arches built dedicated to their achievements. In Rome, the Arch of Septimius Severus commemorates the triumphs over the Parthians and the Arch of Titus was built to commemorate the victories of the emperor, including the Siege of Jerusalem in 70 AD. Centuries later, the Brandenburg Gate in Berlin was erected around 1790 by the King of Prussia to commemorate the successful, albeit temporary, restoration of princely order in Holland during the Batavian Revolution and the Arch de Triomphe in Paris originally celebrated the military successes of Napoleon. Columns were erected in squares to commemorate leaders, from Trajan in Rome to Nelson in London, in the square renamed after the successful naval battle in which Nelson lost his life. The inspiration of these monuments was classical.

In the nineteenth century, when the first war memorials dedicated to loss were erected, the location of the commemorative monument was the town or village the victims originated from. The Franco-Prussian War is seen as the starting date for war memorials in Western Europe. In 1870–71 one empire fell as another was established. Yet the victorious Germans recognized the need for memorials to their dead. In many towns across Germany stone markers are dedicated to those who gave their lives. Across France memorials to honour those who fought the aggressor were erected in the towns and villages where the men came from, back home, miles away from the actual battlegrounds. Many of these war memorials are variations of the classic obelisk, sometimes in a rustic manner, often in a neoclassical fashion, occasionally even neo-baroque. Naming the dead, recognizing the individual in their communal efforts, became increasingly important. Those who are commemorated by the memorial are represented by their names, engraved on stone or bronze plaques, as are the dates of the war, 1870–1871. Occasionally generic symbols occur on these otherwise abstract structures, an eagle representing Germany, and the Gallic rooster embodying the people of France.

Only years before the outbreak of the First World War, the first memorials dedicated to those who gave their lives were introduced in Britain. At the turn of the century, the Anglo-Boer War (1899–1902) shocked the British Empire. After

Above left: Monument to the war victims of the Franco-Prussian War, Holnon, France.

Above right: Boer War memorial in The Promenade, Cheltenham, Gloucestershire.

the war, memorials to the missing soldiers were erected in the towns and cities the recruits fighting in Southern Africa had come from. The Boer War memorial of 1907 in Cheltenham, Gloucestershire, is an example. These memorials express the growing need to commemorate the fallen, to honour the men who gave their lives in a distant place. Boer War memorials often feature a statue of a soldier, a generic representation, occasionally on horseback. The memorial in Crewe is a bronze statue of a soldier placed on top of an obelisk-like column, with the names of the fallen inscribed on the base of the column or engraved on bronze plaques attached to the monument. A common soldier, representing all who lost their lives.

Across the British Empire, memorials dedicated to the memory of soldiers who had lost their lives in South Africa were put up. In Dublin, a monument inspired by Roman triumphal arches was erected at the entrance to St Stephen's Green. Commemorating the battalions of the Royal Dublin Fusiliers that served in South Africa, the memorial by John Howard Pentland has the names of 222 casualties inscribed on the arch. Cecil Rhodes had a memorial erected in Kimberley, Northern

Fusiliers' Arch in Dublin, Ireland, was erected in 1907. The memorial is dedicated to the casualties of the Royal Dublin Fusiliers in the Anglo-Boer War (1899–1902).

Cape province, South Africa, dedicated to those who gave their lives during the Siege of Kimberley (14 October 1899 – 15 February 1900). Rhodes turned to Herbert Baker, an English architect active in South Africa, to design a monument and supported his journey to study ancient Greek memorials. The result was the Honoured Dead Memorial, unveiled in 1904. The tomb of twenty-seven soldiers, the memorial is a neoclassical structure highly influenced by the mausoleum architecture of ancient Greece, such as the Tomb of Theron in Agrigento. Placed on a platform is a massive block containing the space for the actual tombs, on which an open structure of columns, an adaptation of the Tuscan order, is placed. Inscribed are the words:

THIS FOR A CHARGE TO OUR CHILDREN IN SIGN OF THE PRICE WE PAID
THE PRICE WE PAID FOR THE FREEDOM THAT COMES UNSOILED TO
YOUR HAND
READ REVERE AND UNCOVER FOR HERE ARE THE VICTORS LAID
THEY THAT DIED FOR THE CITY BEING SONS OF THE LAND

The text was written by Rudyard Kipling, specifically commissioned by Rhodes for the memorial. It is this commemorative building initiated by Rhodes that can be regarded as the first try-out for the later memorials of the Western Front, of which Sir Herbert Baker would become one of the principle architects commissioned by the Imperial War Graves Commission. The monument that had once celebrated a military victory, such as Nelson's Column in Trafalgar Square of 1843, had developed into a memorial considering loss.

Figurative Representation

Personifications of grief had been represented in memorial sculpture for many centuries. Mourning women or angelic figures adorn commemorative monuments in many churches. When the first war memorials were created in the nineteenth century, the traditional memorial sculpture functioned as an inspiration. The memorials of the Franco-Prussian War took inspiration from classical monuments such as obelisks. But already, occasional figurative elements were added, like mourning female figures and symbolic representations. The Poilu figure that can be found regularly on French memorials is a personification, comparable to the British Tommies, a generic term for all French soldiers from the Trenches. Memorials displaying a Poilu figure can be found in many villages across France. Already, some Boer War memorials had displayed a similar generic soldier representing all who had fallen in combat, notably the memorials in Winsford and Crewe, both in Cheshire. Occasionally British and Commonwealth memorials of the First World War continue this tradition. The Pipers' Memorial in Longueval, France, is an example. An interesting representation of a British soldier and his horse can be found on the Somme, in Chipilly. Here the wounded horse stands for all horses, maybe even all animals, who lost their lives in service. The Canadian Memorial at Vimy in northern France is an example of commemorative architecture with mourners, personifications of all who grieve for loss. Only rarely are persons represented, most notably the Belgian King-Soldier, who, often on horseback, can be found in some Belgian and French cities. The king, of course, becomes a symbol for the resilience of the nation. A more abstract representation of a nation is an animal, the Gallic rooster for France, the caribou for Newfoundland and, more recently, the red dragon for Wales are examples. The bronze sculpture of a caribou, the emblem of the Royal Newfoundland Regiment, was made by the English artist Basil Gotto to commemorate the actions, and sacrifices, of the

A landscape of grief. Sculpture of a mourner overlooking the battlegrounds of Artois. The Canadian National Vimy Memorial, France.

Dominion of Newfoundland. On the Western Front five of these memorials can be found, one in Belgium (Courtrai/Kortrijk) and four in France (Beaumont-Hamel, Gueudecourt, Masnières, Monchy-le-Preux). Of more recent date are the dragons, in Mametz Wood, France, and in the Welsh Memorial Park in Boezinge, Belgium.

The most communicative figurative memorial is undoubtedly that by the sculptress Käthe Kollwitz. A true monument of grief, it represents all mourning mothers, all despairing parents. The Grieving Parents was made in the 1930s and honours the youngest son of Kollwitz, Peter, who died in October 1914. Humbly kneeling in front of the fallen, the grief of all parents is captured perfectly in this cold stone. All relatives and close friends who lost someone dear to them can identify with these two persons, a man and a woman, mourning the loss of their child. True sorrow caught in stone, the Grieving Parents are a universal monument of grief.

Above left: Monument dedicated to the Poilu in Villers-Guislain, France. The term 'Poilu' is an informal word to indicate all infantrymen of the French forces during the First World War. After the war many monuments were erected honouring these men in the towns and villages they came from.

Above right: The Newfoundland Memorial outside Kortrijk, Belgium, a bronze caribou standing on a piece of Newfoundland granite. There are five caribou memorials on the Western Front; the other four are at Masnières, Monchy-le-Preux, Gueudecourt and Beaumont Hamel in France. The sculpture is by Basil Gotto.

Cemeteries

During the first months of the war, preliminary graveyards were established to bury the casualties. Some of these were located in No Man's Land, others behind the front line. The idea of identifying and burying the casualties was a relatively new one; the experiences of the Crimean War (1853–56) and the arrival of the first journalists at the front had substantial influence. Society had changed and people wanted to be informed of what happened at the front. The mass graves near the battlefields that were normal in previous centuries developed into attempts to mark and record all war burials. The role of Sir Fabian Ware in this needs mentioning. Struck by the absence of any official marking and recording of war graves, Ware founded the Graves Registration Commission in 1915, and subsequently the Imperial War Graves Committee in 1917. Simple wooden crosses marked these graves, located in extensions of existing communal cemeteries, in burial grounds near field hospitals or relief stations. At the end of the war there were thousands of provisional cemeteries spread all over Flanders and northern France, and remains of thousands and thousands of unknown and unidentified soldiers were still scattered across the battlegrounds. After considerable debate about repatriation of the bodies,

Bertenacre Military Cemetery, near Flêtre/Vleteren in the French Westhoek. Established as a French military cemetery, casualties from the 36th (Ulster) Division were buried here in summer 1918. After the war, the 115 French and two German burials were relocated to other cemeteries, and British casualties from the preliminary Royal West Sussex Cemetery in nearby Vleteren were relocated to Bertenacre Military Cemetery.

it was decided to create formal cemeteries in Flanders and northern France. The bodies were not to be returned to their homes but would instead be forever buried close to where they had fallen.

Eventually, three model cemeteries were built by the Imperial War Graves Commission as experiments, of which Forceville outside Amiens was agreed upon as the most successful. Designed by Blomfield and Holden, the cemetery at Forceville became an archetype for those assigned by the Imperial War Graves Commission. The cemetery was typified by a uniformity of headstones, placed in a green, almost parklike setting and structured by a green way with a Cross of Sacrifice and a Stone of Remembrance situated on the far ends of it. A small, sober pavilion was placed in a corner of the grounds. Many of the provisional burial grounds were formalized during the years after the war. Some became designated as formal burial places and the bodies and remains of the fallen relocated to vast cemeteries such as Tyne Cot near Passchendale. Not all bodies, however, were repositioned to these collective cemeteries. Many remained in smaller graveyards situated next to communal cemeteries, or even in the countryside in the location of the original burials. These cemeteries give a sense of place, as they were often situated close to the spot where the fallen had lost their lives. Above all, the cemeteries with their crosses of sacrifice have transformed the Western Front into a landscape of remembrance.

The war cemeteries at the Western Front display a wide variety, diverging in size, location and style. In part this has to do with national preferences and with changes in architecture and tastes during the twentieth century. Architecture in the preceding decades had displayed a wide variety of styles, ranging from the neo-baroque to emerging rationalism. This continued in the years after the war. The British and Commonwealth cemeteries were commissioned by the Imperial War Graves

Wooden crosses at a preliminary burial site, Ypres Salient.

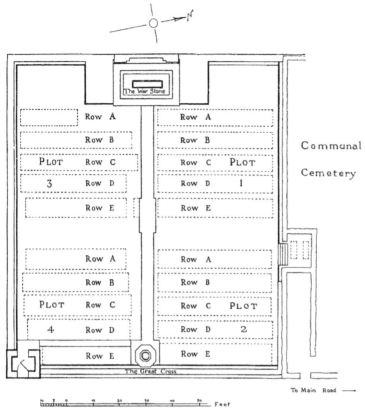

GROUND PLAN OF FORCEVILLE COMMUNAL CEMETERY EXTENSION.

Plan for the Forceville Communal Cemetery Extension by Sir Herbert Baker and Charles Holden. Forceville was one of three experimental cemeteries from which all later war cemeteries derive.

Commission, later known as the Commonwealth War Graves Commission. Similar actions to create permanent war graves were taken by the French and the Germans. Influential in the landscaping of cemeteries in the twentieth century was the Skogskyrkogarden or South Cemetery in Stockholm, designed by Gunnar Asplund and Sigurd Lewertzen in 1915 and created between 1917 and 1920. These grounds can be considered a first attempt to materialize new ideas about graveyard design, concepts that can be found in many later war cemeteries across the world. Central in the design are green slopes, surrounded by woodlands, serving as a meditation zone. A large cross as a visual point is positioned in this part of the grounds. There are several buildings in a functional Nordic classical style, for contemplation. Low walls and some paths are made from rustic stones. The woodlands are used as burial grounds, with the headstones placed in green lawns with trees. Many French war cemeteries, or Nécropoles Nationales as they are called in France, can be considered rational variations of the same concept, with rows of white crosses placed on green slopes surrounded by groups of trees. The Cross, preeminent in the

Stockholm cemetery, is replaced by a flagpole with the French Tricolore attached to it. Saint-Quentin National cemetery is typical.

After the Second World War, Robert Tischler, the official landscape architect of the Volksbundes Deutscher Kriegsgräberfürsorge (VDK) or German War Graves Committee, was appointed to redesign several war cemeteries in Belgium and France. Langemark German War Cemetery and Menen German War Cemetery – with nearly 48,000 burials, the largest war cemetery of the First World War in Belgium – are typical examples of the woodland type of burial ground design and lack the formality typical of so many other military cemeteries. These woodlands with simple crosses and monuments expressing grief have become outdoor spaces for remembrance. Part of the landscaping of many war cemeteries is the planting. Trees can be planted, giving a verticality to the grounds, as boundaries or accentuations. In both French and British war cemeteries roses are occasionally planted on the graves. The flowering red roses juxtaposed with the white headstones or crosses seem to recall the sacrifices made by those who gave their blood and lives.

In some cemeteries the headstones appear to be placed in flowerbeds, transforming the burial grounds into commemorative gardens. Many of these burial grounds are enclosed by a wall or on occasions a hedge; often, in a way, gardens were structured in cubicles. There were walls of various heights, in materials reflecting the surroundings: brick walls in the polders of Flanders – Morbecque is an example – and rubble walls in the hamlets of the Aisne, as in Bellenglise. Significant in the landscaping of many British and Commonwealth war cemeteries in Flanders and France was the influence of the Arts & Crafts Movement. Many architects involved in the creation of the war cemeteries were inspired by the Movement; William Harrison Cowlishaw springs

Sequehart British
Cemetery, France.

Red roses at the Douaumont
war cemetery near Verdun.

Beaurevoir British
Cemetery, France.

to mind. A juxtaposition of abstract forms with the combination of rustic regional
materials, the use of parterres to overcome problems of difference in altitudes in some
burial grounds – especially the smaller cemeteries – reveals the influence of garden
design, especially the fruitful association of Lutyens and Jekyll. This landscaping has
softened the harsh neoclassical forms of some monuments. Even the most rigid of
formal designs reveal an understanding of the landscape, with the cemeteries and
memorials becoming requisites in a scene. Lutyens places his Thiepval Memorial
in the countryside of Picardy in the way Hawksmoor put his Mausoleum in the
grounds of Castle Howard, carefully positioning this memorial (1729–40) in the
setting of North Yorkshire. Treating the countryside as a landscape, memorials and
cemeteries intentionally become part of the countryside, transforming it. This is
scenography shaping the countryside into vast landscapes of memories, placing the
cemeteries and memorials in the countryside as monuments in a large country estate.

The English baroque had been inspirational for many architects in the decades before the war; the spirits of Vanbrugh (1664–1726) and Hawksmoor (1661–1736) are felt in the designs and the positioning of the memorials and cemeteries. Cabaret Rouge Memorial and Cemetery in Souchez is a convincing demonstration, especially the triumphant entrance gate, and the Vis-en-Artois Memorial and Cemetery, designed by John Reginald Truelove (1886–1942), is a landmark in the manner of the English baroque. Noticeably more restrained are the designs by Charles Holden, who chose compositions of rectangular volumes and powerful piled-up masses. Grand Seraucourt British Cemetery is typical. At Messines, the well-suited unadorned neoclassicism of the New Zealand Memorial becomes the awakening of a new rationalism. Here, Charles Holden shows an unassuming architecture of remembrance. Ancient Greek architecture seems to have influenced the Pozières Memorial, yet the entrance gate is an exercise in Wrenaissance. Most of the smaller cemeteries, however, are executed in an English vernacular.

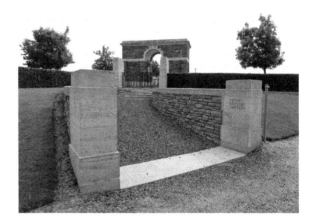

The entrance and gate to Pernes British Cemetery, Pas-de-Calais, France.

Thiepval Memorial to the Missing by Sir Edwin Lutyens, positioned in the landscape of Picardy.

The most defining architectural elements in war cemeteries are the Cross of Sacrifice and the Stone of Remembrance. The first crosses at the Western Front were erected soon after the first victims had fallen. Often made of wood and later replaced, these crosses marked the locations of where the officers and men had died. Flemish Catholic nationalists were commemorated by a Celtic cross designed by the artist Joe English, a draftsman from Bruges of Irish descent. The Imperial War Graves Commission, today the Commonwealth War Graves Commission, asked Sir Reginald Blomfield to design a Cross of Sacrifice in 1918. His design, an elongated cross free of stylistic connotations, is intentionally abstract and impersonal. A bronze longsword, with the blade down, is attached to it, sometimes on both sides. Typically the cross has an octagonal base. First unveiled in 1920, this design has become the archetype of the British war memorial and can be found around the world. With the sword pointing towards the grounds, the cross becomes strongly fixed to the site, in many cases marking the spot of sacrifice. An abstract tribute, the Cross of Sacrifice is one of the most recognisable memorials and a prevailing symbol.

The Cross of Sacrifice, designed by Sir Reginald Blomfield. Montay British Cemetery, France.

The Stone of Remembrance was designed to be used in First World War cemeteries commemorating 1,000 or more; however, it can also be found in many smaller cemeteries. An abstract design, the memorial can be interpreted as simultaneously a cenotaph, a stone tomb and an altar dedicated to those who gave their lives. It was designed by Sir Edwin Lutyens. In recent years the Stone has been interpreted by some authors as an altar celebrating the sacrifice of soldiers. The positioning of the Stone of Remembrance at some cemeteries can enhance such understanding. Appreciating the War Stone as part of memorial typology, it is analogous to the Canadian commemorative blocks. The Stone is a visual sign, an architectural focus giving structure to commemorative sites, and functions as a common tomb, a stone sarcophagus. Indeed, Lutyens is also the architect of the Cenotaph Memorial in Whitehall. On the stone, words chosen by Rudyard Kipling from the biblical Wisdom of Sirach are engraved – 'Their Name Liveth For Ever More' – emphasizing the meaning of the Stone of Remembrance as a cenotaph to all who lost their lives. Like the Cross of Sacrifice by Blomfield, Lutyens's Stone of Remembrance has become part of British war memorials and today can be found all over the world. However, both memorials were first designed for commemoration of the war casualties of the First World War.

The Stone of Remembrance, common tomb and cenotaph of the fallen. Savy British Cemetery, France. The words 'Their Name Liveth For Evermore' from the Wisdom of Sirach were chosen by Rudyard Kipling. The Stone of Remembrance was designed by Sir Edwin Lutyens.

Architecture of Remembrance

The intention of any memorial is to prevent a progress of forgetting. Materializing the intangible concept of absence is the principal task of the architect. To design the cemeteries and memorials, artists and architects were commissioned or competitions were organised. The French monuments are mostly the result of competitions. In 1920 the Canadian Battlefields Memorials Commission was established, which organised competitions for the eight Canadian memorial sites on the Western Front. Square blocks, commemorating significant battles by the Canadian Expeditionary Force, were placed in Bourlon, Courcelette, Dury, Le Quesnel, Zonnebeke and in Passendale. The design of these granite blocks is identical and the inscriptions are related to the site. In 1921 the design by Walter Seymour Allward was selected by the Commission as the winner of the competition for a Canadian National Memorial; eventually Vimy Ridge near Lens, France, was chosen as the location. The Imperial War Graves Commission, today known as the CWGC, assigned Sir Herbert Baker, Sir Reginald Blomfield and Sir Edwin Lutyens as the principle architects to design the British and Commonwealth memorials and cemeteries. Later, Charles Holden was appointed as the fourth.

All four were prominent architects from the Edwardian Age, and three received a knighthood. Between 1923 and 1938 numerous memorials were created for the Imperial War Graves Commission, dedicated to those who had no known grave. These memorials show a continuation of Edwardian architecture, but as a consequence also show the lack of a single style. The classical idiom remains the principle inspiration for all designers, architects and sculptors, the output ranging from styles reviving the

Pozières Cemetery and Memorial to the Missing, a dignified composition of classical features recalling ancient Greek architecture.

A portrait of
Charles Holden
by Benjamin
Nelson.

English Baroque to an approach inspired by the Arts & Crafts Movement. By using
the Cross of Sacrifice and, to a lesser extent, the Stone of Remembrance as principal
design features, a certain degree of uniformity was achieved. The disposition of these
two elements, however, shows the different opinions of the architects. Some chose a
formality to design the grounds, a rigid symmetry with a green way and the cross as
ultimate culmination. Especially in combination with the Stone of Remembrance,
some of these war cemeteries can have the appearance of open-air chapels. Other
designers have been inspired by the location of the cemetery, following the landscape
and deliberately positioning the Cross in the grounds asymmetrically.

Herbert Baker (1862–1946), an Englishman who had worked in South Africa at
Cecil Rhodes's suggestion between 1893 and 1912, was later appointed with Lutyens
to design the principal buildings in Imperial Delhi. South Africa House in Trafalgar
Square is one of his best known accomplishments. Previously, Baker had designed
the Honoured Dead Memorial dedicated to the fallen of the Anglo-Boer War in
Kimberley, Northern Cape province. A mausoleum in the neoclassical style, with
an inscription by Kipling, the Kimberley memorial can be considered a prototype
for the later British and Commonwealth memorials of the Western Front. In 1923
Baker received a knighthood. Reginald Blomfield (1856–1942), one of the great
architects of the Edwardian period, much admired the works of Sir Christopher
Wren. His books, lectures and buildings have contributed immeasurably to the
British classical architecture of the Edwardian age. Much of his accomplishments
were inspired by the English Baroque. Among his best known works is Regent Street,
London. Blomfield was knighted in 1919. Charles Holden (1875–1960), born in

Bolton, Lancashire, was perhaps the most modern of these architects involved with the designs of war graves, and strongly believed in the concept of 'fitness for purpose'. Holden worked for the Imperial War Graves Commission between 1918 and 1928; in 1920 he became one of the four principal architects, and is responsible for sixty-nine cemeteries on the Western Front. Later, Holden became known for his Tube stations on the Piccadilly line. A master of an unadorned style of architecture, stripped of unnecessary decorations, he was never tempted to design palaces for the dead. Holden declined a knighthood twice. William Cowlishaw (1869–1957), who worked with Charles Holden at the Commission, came from the Arts & Crafts Movement and was inspired by William Morris. He is best known for designing The Cloisters in Letchworth Garden City. Perhaps the best known of these men today is Lutyens. A great architect from the Edwardian period, Sir Edwin Lutyens displayed a mastery of architecture in its numerous manifestations, from garden design, in cooperation with Gertrude Jekyll, to the shaping of Imperial Delhi. A preoccupation with the English baroque – Lutyens liked the term Wrenaissance – appears to be the common denominator. The creation of different scenographies to host different occasions means the architect becomes a stage designer adapting the setting to its function. His work for the Imperial War Graves Commission is significant. Both the Cenotaph in Whitehall and the Thiepval Memorial in France are by Lutyens, as well as many war cemeteries and memorials on the Western Front. The larger designs such as the Arras memorials reveal the influence of figures such as Vanbrugh and Hawksmoor; in his designs for the smaller cemeteries, his previous cooperation with Jekyll is ubiquitous. One may accuse Lutyens of a keen interest in grand designs and of glorifying the fallen, as some authors have; the formality of his designs is an attempt to give back some of the dignity these men lost during the hardships of the war. In his designs, Lutyens honours their sacrifice, knows when the monumental scale is appropriate and understands the meaning of architecture.

In the years after the war, the need was recognised not just for cemeteries to bury the bodies and remains of the war casualties, but also for memorials. Intentions for these memorials can be various. Some are monuments to recall actions or events. There are many obelisks constructed on the Western Front to commemorate actions of regiments or divisions, such as the 62nd West Riding Division Memorial outside Havrincourt near Cambrai, France. A tragic memorial can be found in St Juliaan, Flanders, which is dedicated to the first victims of gas attacks during the First World War. Many thousands of casualties could not be registered and identified and the creation of memorials as a place of remembrance to the missing was felt to be a necessity. Many of these memorials to the missing are connected to war cemeteries. And finally there was the construction of national war monuments as sites

The Cenotaph, designed by Sir Edwin Lutyens, in Whitehall.

of public mourning. Perhaps the Ossuary of Douaumont near Verdun is the most comprehensive example of a memorial to the victims of the First World War. A vast war cemetery is located in the former battlegrounds. Woods grow where once villages stood. A building was constructed overlooking the vast site, consisting of a memorial hall displaying the names of the fallen, a central tower as a lantern and a chapel. Beneath the memorial hall is the actual ossuary. This French national war monument, designed by Leon Azéma, was established shortly after the war in 1919 and completed in 1932. Monumental architecture such as these memorials becomes a site of pilgrimage and a place of public and private remembrance. Recurrent typologies of these national monuments include the tower, the memorial hall, the chapel and the gateway. The tower as a lantern and indicator is found at several major memorials, from the Australian National Memorial at Villers-Bretonneux to the gargantuan cross of the Flemish Memorial near Diksmuide. The Yser Tower is a combination of a cross and a tower. Lutyens' Australian memorial is a tower in a neoclassical style with stairs in a curious location recalling the paper architecture of Piranesi's *Carceri d'Invenzione*. The silhouettes of both memorials are remarkably similar. Both can be interpreted as lanterns of peace. The Ulster Tower in Thiepval and the round tower in Messines are interesting; by their distinct architecture, they represent nations in a foreign field. Here the architecture is deliberately neither an abstraction nor timeless but a connection to the homelands. This kind of intended national style in memorials is, however, found only sporadically. Most memorial architecture remains strongly rooted in the classical tradition, with differences in interpretation. The King Albert

Monument in Nieuwpoort is an example of what can be called an art deco monument, or a modernised classicism, on a circular plan. A similar unadorned classicism is found in Charles Holden's memorials and funerary architecture. An example is his New Zealand Memorial in Polygon Wood near Zonnebeke, Flanders. Two memorial pavilions are connected by a covered pathway or stoa. The stoa, or cloisters as Lutyens describes them on his plans, is a classic architectural intervention to shape space and structure, place and movement. Some of these stoas are placed on only one side of the cemetery, others have a U-shape and are reminiscent of the ancient Pergamum Altar. The war cemetery thus becomes a chapel of remembrance, dedicated to martyrs of the First World War. An example can be found in Pozières. Visiting these war cemeteries becomes a pilgrimage, as in ancient times, to honour the sacrifices.

The Douaumont ossuary, designed by Leon Azéma, near Verdun. Beneath the building are the skeletal remains of 130,000 unidentified war casualties.

The Ulster Tower Memorial.

At Arras, Lutyens creates a setting with cloisters and the Cross of Sacrifice and the Stone of Remembrance positioned in an ecclesiastical setting, evoking religious architecture. Also, other cemeteries and memorials strongly recall open air chapels, by their design and especially by the positioning of the Cross of Sacrifice and Stone of Remembrance. The French and Belgians have created many chapels along the Western Front dedicated to all victims of the First World War. Typically these are located on the sites of former chapels or churches destroyed during the war, such as the Chapel of Our Lady in Stuivekenskerke. Many of these were reconstructions of the chapel which had been destroyed during the war, rededicated to the war victims. A chapel in a Romanesque-Byzantine revivalist style, designed by Louis Marie Cordonnier, inaugurated in 1925, replaced an original chapel of the eighteenth century on this location. Today it is part of the French Nécropole Nationale of Notre-Dame-de-Lorette. The Ypres League anticipated the erection of an Anglican memorial church in Ypres in the 1920s. Land was given by the municipality of Ypres, in the near vicinity of the local cathedral, and the church dedicated to St George would be inaugurated in 1929. Designed by Sir Reginald Bloomfield, the church is a remarkable combination of Flemish and British architecture, resulting in a unique building. It is part of the Diocese of Europe in the Church of England. The interior is almost like a memorial hall, adorned with commemorative plaques and regimental flags, and with windows filled with commemorative stained glass. Many other churches and cathedrals have similar memorials of the First World War, memorial plaques near the main entrance or stained glass windows. Chapels can be regarded as a religious kind of memorial hall. The most intriguing of these memorial halls is the one in Ypres, at first sight a victory arch in the classical tradition.

Arches have been built to commemorate victories since Roman times. The Menin Gate Memorial to the Missing appears to be part of this centuries-old tradition of celebrating a military triumph. Yet, passing through the gate and entering the rebuilt medieval town of Ypres, the difference with Constantine's Arch in Rome or the Brandenburg Gate in Berlin couldn't be greater. The gateway provides entrance to a hall with the names of the missing written all over it. The Menin Gate is a monument of grief. As the destroyed historic centre of Ypres was being reconstructed, arguably becoming itself a memorial, the Menin Gate was not rebuilt but replaced by a new structure. Designed by Blomfield, the new gate became a memorial to the missing of the Ypres Salient, a place of remembrance for those who lost their lives and have no known grave. The reasons for choosing this gate as the location for a war monument were related to the position it holds and the view towards the belfry and Cloth Hall. Architecturally, this memorial is part of the urban fabric. It is not a space that keeps out daily life, an interior that isolates itself

Thiepval Memorial to the Missing of the Somme.

in a monument as Aldo Rossi understood the meaning of a monument. Menin Gate has become known for the Last Post ceremony which takes place every day inside the memorial hall and has become part of daily life. This ritual has grown from within the local community. During this daily ceremony, the building is transformed from a passage way to a place of remembrance. The gate becomes a place for the communal commemoration of grief. Gateways form entrances to monumental cemeteries such as Pozières and Cabaret-Rouge military cemeteries. Here, the gate has a function as a monumental entrance building; passing through the gate is part of the experience. It is inviting to compare some of these gates, especially those similar to Pozières Cemetery, in the tradition of triumph arches, dedicated to the glory of those who gave their lives. One can be tempted to see the Thiepval Memorial as a wonderfully dislocated monument, one of the best archways in architecture yet without an urban context to give the structure meaning. There is no culmination of a processional way, as is the case in Paris or Berlin or even Ypres, and the idea of passing through the gate, the purifying transit trough purgatory that is the procession at Ypres, is completely absent. This memorial is an enormous canopy over a common tomb which is the Stone of Remembrance. It is a monument to sacrifice, an attempt to give back some dignity to those men who gave their lives during the Somme battles. In a way it is reminiscent of the other great memorial by Lutyens, the Cenotaph in Whitehall. Both are designed as scenography to stage memorial observations.

A Landscape of Memories

Soon after the war had ended, the first visitors came to see the remnants of the battlefields. People wanted to see for themselves the places where their loved ones were during the years of the war, where their relatives had suffered and lost their lives. Already in the first years after the war had ended, visitors came to see the places their loved ones had been, to see for themselves the trenches, the craters, and the war graves. Death Trench in Flanders was one of the earliest sites to attract visitors, receiving the first sightseers in the first years after the war. Some battles have become part of our collective memory. Visiting these battlegrounds becomes a pilgrimage. They give a sense of place where the memory of the war remains tangible. The craters left by mines or bombs, the deformed landscape revealing traces of trenches and shelling, a communicative site and a place of memories. The Battle of Messines in Flanders, better known as the Mines Battle, is still visible in the landscape. Newfoundland Memorial Park in Beaumont Hamel is a comprehensive domain comprising remnants of the battlegrounds, smaller memorials and war cemeteries. Monuments dedicated to the actions of divisions, traces of trenches and shelling, crosses of sacrifice to mark the spots: the place strongly evokes the battlefields of the Somme. A destination of modern pilgrimage, the Newfoundland park has become one of the most visited sites at the Western Front, expressing the desire to visit landscapes of memories. The war memorial has developed from monumental structures of the inter-war period into parks consisting of tangible fragments of the battlefields.

All over Flanders, Liberty Trees, or Peace Trees, were planted to commemorate the Armistice of 1918. Some of these living memorials are still there, in villages and towns across Flanders from Oostvleteren to Nieuwkerke. Often these living memorials were located in a public place near the war memorial, as is the case in Machelen. Planting commemorative trees was not a new development, but rather a continuation of a longer tradition. In 1830 remembrance trees had been planted to celebrate Belgian independence. The memorial tree in Voormezele near Ypres was planted in 1968 to mark the Golden Jubilee of the Armistice. Today, the tradition has been revived and over 200 remembrance trees will be planted in Flanders to mark the centennial of the Armistice. An interesting new project is the creation of New Polygon Wood, including five trees representing five nations associated with the fighting in Polygon Wood, which played a significant part in the tragic Battle of Passchendaele. A central part of the new wood will be a forest of poppies, this delicate flower and sturdy symbol transforming these former battlegrounds into a contemporary memorial, a field of poppies, a moving place of remembrance.

Lochnagar Mine Crater, one of the most visited memorial sites of the Somme battlefields.

THE YSER AND THE
YPRES SALIENT

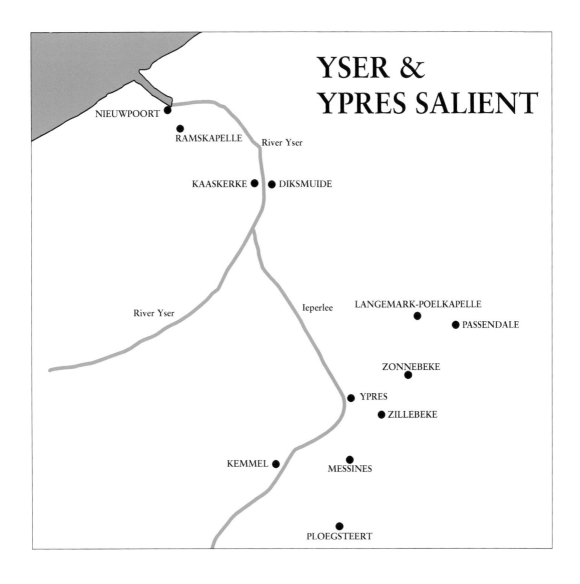

**YSER &
YPRES SALIENT**

NIEUWPOORT ●

● RAMSKAPELLE

River Yser

KAASKERKE ● ● DIKSMUIDE

Ieperlee   LANGEMARK-POELKAPELLE ●

                                      ● PASSENDALE

River Yser

ZONNEBEKE ●

● YPRES

● ZILLEBEKE

KEMMEL ●   ● MESSINES

● PLOEGSTEERT

In Flanders Fields.
Tyne Cot, the largest
Commonwealth War
Graves Commission
cemetery in the world,
outside Passendale.

Belgium was invaded in early August 1914 after refusing passage for German troops.
The advance of the Imperial Germany was halted in October that year at the Yser,
a modest stream in the west of Flanders, in what became known as the Battle of the
Yser. Belgian forces held the front until 1918. Along the River Yser several memorials
commemorating the casualties of the Yser front can be found. The first and foremost
Belgian memorial is dedicated to King Albert and is situated on a strategic complex
of waterways in the medieval port town of Nieuwpoort, where the Yser ends in the
North Sea. A complex of locks, called the Ganzepoot [Goose Foot], controlled the
water in the polders surrounding Nieuwpoort. This was used to turn the land into a
muddy, watery mess, halting the German advance. A key role in the Belgian defence
was played by Albert I, who became known as the King-Soldier. After the war many
memorials were erected to honour his role as King, and as such the monument is not
only dedicated to personal significance but to Belgian resilience. The most prominent
monument is undoubtedly the one in Nieuwpoort. Overlooking the Goose Foot,
which had played its part in the Battle of the Yser, the monument consists of a bronze
figure of the King on horseback placed within a circular edifice built from a yellow
brick typical of the Yser region. The structure was designed by Julien De Ridder and
the statue of the King-Soldier on horseback is by the sculptor Karel Aubroeck. It was
built in 1938, a few years after the tragic death of the King in Marche-les-Dames,
and unveiled by his children and grandchildren. After renovation the memorial was
reopened in 2014 for the centenary commemorations. Today, the King's memorial
is part of a larger monument called Westfront Nieuwpoort. Beneath the terrace and
the memorial a visitors' centre was created, hosting permanent exhibitions exploring
the polders and the water. An impressive panorama of the Battle of the Yser, 1914, is
projected on a large screen.

King Albert of Belgium on horseback. The memorial was unveiled in 1938, after the tragic death of the King in Marche-les-Dames, by his wife, Queen Elisabeth, and his sons King Leopold III and Prince Charles, Count of Flanders.

Memorial dedicated to the King-Soldier Albert I of Belgium and all Belgian soldiers of the First World War, Nieuwpoort.

In front of the King Albert I memorial is the British Nieuport Memorial. This memorial, designed by William Binnie, is reminiscent of the Cenotaph in Whitehall and lists the names of 547 British officers. The three lions couchant were made by Charles Sargeant Jagger. The British memorial was unveiled in 1928. Just outside Nieuwpoort on the N367, and only 500 meters from the Goose Foot, the Ramscapelle Road Military Cemetery can be found. It was first established in 1917; after the war, the cemetery was altered and extended to a design by Sir Edwin Lutyens. At Ramscapelle Cemetery, 841 Commonwealth soldiers who gave their lives at the Yser front in 1917 are remembered. A Stone of Remembrance, commissioned by the Imperial War Graves Commission and designed by Sir Edwin Lutyens, is placed opposite a Cross of Sacrifice, giving structure to this graveyard. Of the other memorials near Nieuwpoort, the Belgian Military Cemetery is worth noting, commemorating 632 fallen, of which 400 have not been identified. The village of Stuyvekenskerke on the River Yser is the location of a memorial chapel dedicated to Our Lady of Victory. This chapel, a private initiative by M. Lekeux, commemorates 40,000 casualties of the First World War on the Yser front and was inaugurated in

1925. In 1955 stained glass windows were presented. Surrounding the chapel are forty-one stones commemorating forty-one regiments. The location of this chapel was chosen because of the historic church tower, now a ruin, which was used as a watch tower during the war. An interesting memorial and one of the first sites of the First World War to attract visitors is the Dodengang, or Trench of Death in English, in Kaaskerke. Located on the Yser canal, the Trench of Death is a preserved section of a trench which was part of the Yser. Only a few hundred meters upstream, the tallest and best known memorial of the Yser Front is located, the remarkable Yser Tower. This monumental structure stands 84 meters tall and commemorates all Flemish casualties of the First World War. It has the shape of a cross and contains five letters, representing the motto Alles Voor Vlaanderen, Vlaanderen Voor Kristus ['All for Flanders, Flanders for Christ']. The tower is a monument to peace, with the words 'No More War' on the base of the tower in four languages: English, French, German and Flemish. The complex consists of the Yser Tower, the Pax Gate of peace, the ruins of the preceding tower – destroyed during the Second World War – and a crypt. Of interest are the headstones, designed by Joe English of Bruges.

Houthulst Belgian Military Cemetery was established in 1923 on a battlefield where fighting had taken place on 28 September 1918. Among the burials are eighty-one Italian prisoners of war who had been used by the Germans as human shields.

The Trench of Death, near Diksmuide/Dixmude. Attracting visitors since 1919, the Trench of Death was one of the earliest visitor sites on the Western Front.

To the north of Vladslo on the N363 towards Wijnendale is the Vladslo German Military Cemetery, a typical woodland cemetery which contains the remains of over 25,000 troops, of which 3,233 are wartime burials. The names of the burials are engraved on granite plates lying in the grass, as part of the redesign of the grounds of 1956 when German war casualties were relocated to Vladslo German Military Cemetery. It is the location of *The Grieving Parents*, a pair of figures by the sculptress Käthe Kollwitz. The sculpture is a moving memorial to all sons, all offspring, that were killed during the First World War. Kollwitz made it in memory of her son Peter, who was killed during the first Battle of Ypres. Just outside Houthulst, on the N301 towards Poelkapelle, the Houthulst Belgian Military Cemetery is located. It was designed by Blondeau and Moreau of Bruges and was unveiled in 1925. Of the 1,804 casualties buried at Houthulst, eighty-one are of Italian nationality. On 4 May 1915 Italy joined the coalition of Allied forces against the German and Austrian-Hungarian empires. The Italian headstones at Houthulst Military Cemetery recollect their participation on the Western Front.

The town of Poelkapelle was recaptured by the British on 4 October 1917, by the 11th Division, during the Third Battle of Ypres. Designed by Charles Holden, the Poelcapelle Military Cemetery was built after the war, in 1919, and contains the remains of over 7,000 men, of which 6,230 have not been identified, who gave their lives in battle in the region of Poelkapelle. The cemetery is surrounded by a brick wall and a Stone of Remembrance is placed opposite a Cross of Sacrifice. It is situated on the N313 to Westrozebeke. Placed in a roundabout near the village church of Poelkapelle is a memorial honouring Georges Guynemer, a top fighter ace and French national hero, who fell in 1917 outside the village. On top of the column is a bronze representation of a flying stork, symbolising the Escadron de Chasse

Grieving Parents by Käthe Kollwitz, Vladslo German War Cemetery. It was made in commemoration of her eighteen-year-old son Peter, who was killed in 1914.

1/2 Cigognes (Stork Squadron). In the near vicinity is the Tank Memorial, Ypres Salient, inaugurated on 10 October 2009, commemorating all victims of the actions of tanks during the First World War. Poelkapelle had been the location of tank warfare in 1917, but many British tanks were too heavy for the muddy fields of western Flanders and got stuck. After the war, the landscape between Poelkapelle and St-Juliaan was a graveyard of tanks. One of these was relocated to Poelkapelle and placed in the village centre, attracting many visitors, until it was dismantled by the Germans in 1941. The village of Langemark was on the Western Front from October 1914. It came into German hands after the chlorine gas attack of April 1915 during the Second Battle of Ypres. The Langemark Myth became part of the 1930s German narrative. Just to the north of the village is located the German Military Cemetery, containing the remains of 44,000 German and two British soldiers. Central is the Comrades' Grave, containing almost 25,000 unidentified troops, with in the back the monument of *The Mourning Soldiers*, a bronze made by Emil Krieger. This was originally closer to the memorial hall and was moved to the back during the redesign of the 1950s. On the N313 from Westrozebeke to Ieper and the road from Langemark to Zonnebeke, a grey stone memorial is located in a green setting. *The Brooding Soldier*, as the memorial is called, is an exceptional tribute, both in function and design, and commonly known in west Flanders as 'The Canadian'. The design by Frederick Chapman Clemesha won the 1920 competition. It was revealed in 1923 in presence of HRH the Duke of Brabant and Prince Arthur, Duke of Connaught and Strathearn. The grey stone column on a square plan merges with a statue representing a Canadian soldier. It commemorates the thousands who lost their lives during the first poison gas attack, on 22 April 1915, by the German imperial army at Sint-Juliaan/Saint-Julien, marking the beginning of the Second Battle of Ypres. Commemorating the Welsh men and women, the memorial grounds near Boezinge were opened in August 2014, in a location associated with the Welsh units during the Battle of Passchendaele (1917). It was the first Welsh memorial in Flanders. The initiator was Erwin Ureel, who laid out the general design. A bronze dragon, painted red, surmounts a cromlech or dolmen made out of large grey boulders that come from Pontypridd. These dolmens are ancient burial places which can be found in Wales.

The Battle of Passchendaele, also known as the Third Battle of Ypres, has become part of collective memory. Between July and November 1917 thousands of casualties fell in a campaign that remains controversial. To the north-west of the town, the Passchendaele New British Cemetery can be found. Designed by Charles Holden, over 2,100 soldiers are buried here, of which 1,600 remain unidentified. A more recent white stone memorial decorated with the crest of the Province of West

Mourning figures by Emil Krieger, Langemark German Cemetery.

Langemark German Cemetery.

Flanders reads 'Eind offensief Passendale 28 september 1918' and commemorates the final offensive before the Armistice of 11 November 1918. Inside the church of St Audomarus in Passendale town, stained glass windows honour the battles of the 66th Division, British Expeditionary Force. A bronze memory plaque reading, 'This window is dedicated to the memory of the 66th Division British Expeditionary Force 1914–1918,' is placed on the wall. Just outside Passendale is the Passendale Canadian Memorial, one of six similar memorials erected by the Canadian Battlefield Monument Commission. The other five can be found at Hill 62 (Ypres) in Belgium, and Courcelette, Le Quesnel, Dury and Bourlon Wood in France. The words on the base of the cube read: 'Honour to the Canadians who on the fields of Flanders and of France fought in the cause of the allies with sacrifice and devotion.'

Tank near Passendale/
Passchendaele.

Between Passendale and Zonnebeke, west of the N303, is the location of Tyne
Cot Cemetery. The Tyne Cot Commonwealth War Graves Cemetery and Memorial
to the Missing, forever a piece of the United Kingdom, were designed by Sir Herbert
Baker and unveiled in 1922 by Sir Gilbert Dyett. The restrained composition of this
memorial and cemetery in this emotionally loaded location shows the competence of
Baker. The first cemetery of 1917 was taken by the enemy in April 1918 and finally
recaptured by Belgian troops in late September 1918. Recognizing the sacrifices made
by the British defending and liberating Belgium, the grounds in which the memorial
and cemetery are located were given to the United Kingdom by King Albert I of
Belgium. Tyne Cot, probably the most impressive memorial site in the region, is
the largest Commonwealth Military Cemetery in the world. The remains of nearly
12,000 soldiers, of which 8,369 are unnamed, are buried here. The origin of the
name of this cemetery and memorial comes from the Northumberland Fusiliers, who
noted a resemblance between the German concrete pill boxes (bunkers) in the area
and workers' cottages in Tyneside. There are several memorials in Passendale today.
Behind Tyne Cot, a memorial honouring the Sherwood Foresters was established in
2009. The Regiment of the Sherwood Foresters was founded in 1881 and eventually
merged in 1970 with the Worcestershire Regiment to create the 2nd Battalion the
Mercian Regiment. To commemorate the activities of the Sherwood Foresters at
the Western Front, a new memorial was created near the entrance of the Tyne Cot
visitor centre. Also behind Tyne Cot is a memorial dedicated to the the King's Own
Yorkshire Light Infantry, which was unveiled in 2007 during the commemorations
of the ninetieth anniversary of the Third Battle of Ypres.

South of Zonnebeke is Polygon Wood, an ancient forest which was completely
destroyed during the First World War as a result of the strategic location of the
woods. Only on 28 September 1918 were the woods finally recaptured by the

Right: Tyne Cot
Commonwealth War Graves
Cemetery and Memorial to the
Missing, Passendale.

Below: Graves in the Flemish
mud, Ypres Salient.

9th Scottish Division. Today, a new wood is being planted, a wood of trees and a forest of poppies to commemorate those who lost their lives in the fields of Flanders. Buttes New British Cemetery (NZ) Cemetery and Memorial, one of seven at the Western Front dedicated to the missing from New Zealand, is located at Polygon Wood. The memorial, designed by Charles Holden, commemorates 378 men from the New Zealand Division who gave their lives and have no known grave in the region. The Buttes New British Cemetery contains the remains of over 2,000 Commonwealth officers and men. Opposing the neoclassical memorial portico, a Stone of Remembrance is placed. Nearby is the Polygon Wood Cemetery, again designed by Charles Holden, honouring 107 losses. Centrally placed in the grounds is a tall Cross of Sacrifice. An obelisk dedicated to the 5th Australian division in

Zonnebeke was unveiled by HRH the Prince of Wales in 1932. A grey stone column on a square plan was erected to honour the Princess Patricia's Canadian Light Infantry, a notable circular memorial, dedicated in 1964. In 2007 a stone Celtic cross was unveiled on Frezenberg Hill outside Zonnebeke, commemorating all Scots and those of Scottish descent who gave their lives at the Western Front.

After four years of war, the medieval city of Ypres was left in ruins. Most of it was meticulously reconstructed in defiance of its annihilation. The reconstructed Cloth Hall with its belfry, the largest secular building of the thirteenth century, was the background for the 2017 remembrance events, an impressive remembrance service attended by HRH the Duke and Duchess of Cambridge and the King and Queen of Belgium. As the Cloth Hall served as a background to the show, the procession proceeded through towards the Menin Gate. Of all memorials in Flanders, the Menin Gate has become the most recognized. The building was conceived as a Hall of Memory to the Missing of the Ypres Salient as well as a passageway. The names of over 50,000 troops whose bodies have not been recovered or identified are represented on stone panels. In West Flanders, remains of missing soldiers are found regularly to this day; names are removed from the panels if the bodies can be identified. In 2017 the limestone lions that adorned the original pre-war Menin Gate returned from Canberra, where they are part of the Australian War Memorial. The temporary return of the lions, which were presented to Australia by the town of Ypres in 1936, was celebrated as a homecoming.

To commemorate the 500,000 British troops that gave their lives in the Ypres Salient, a memorial church was built on land provided by the municipality of Ypres, a location in the town centre not far from St Martin's Cathedral. The task of designing the building was given to Sir Reginald Bloomfield, who also designed

The New Zealand Memorial to the Missing, Polygon Wood, commemorating the 378 soldiers of the New Zealand Division who have no known grave. The restrained classicism is typical of the work of Charles Holden.

Right: The names of the 54,395 missing of the Ypres Salient, Menin Gate.

Below: Bird's eye view of Ypres, 1918.

the Menin Gate Memorial. In 1927 the first stone was laid by Field Marshal Lord Plumer in a ceremony attended by King Albert I of Belgium. Two years later the church was dedicated by the Bishop of Fulham. Saint George's Memorial Church is a Belgian national monument. An interesting combination of English and Flemish building styles has resulted in a unique monument. The interior is the site of many memorials to regiments, associations and individuals, with walls of brass plaques and flags. During the Second World War, the people of Ypres hid the contents of the church for safe-keeping. Although part of the Anglican church province, services are ecumenical. The service on Armistice Day, 11 November, has particular significance and seats for the service are allocated by ticket. In September 2017, a ring of eight change-ringing bells was placed in the tower, and locals were introduced to the English tradition of bell-ringing.

Of the many memorials and war cemeteries in and around Ypres, some are worth mentioning. A stained glass rose window in the Cathedral was presented by the British troops to King Albert I, and inaugurated in 1938 by his son King Leopold III. It honours all victims of the First World War. Close to the Menin Gate, a poem by Edmund Blunden is displayed. The Belgian Memorial, against a wall close to the Cloth Hall, is dedicated to military and civilian casualties of the First World War. It was designed by Jules Coomans, great architect of the reconstruction of Ypres, and is locally known as the Ypres Fury.

Hooge Crater Cemetery on the N8 from Ypres to Menin/Menen is the final resting place of over 5,900 soldiers whose remains came from several military cemeteries in Geluwe, Geluveld, Zonnebeke and Zillebeke. It was originally the site of the Chateau de Hooge, which had been used by the British as a divisional headquarters; both the house and village of Hooge were completely destroyed. A Stone of Remembrance is placed in a circular green, the Cross of Sacrifice behind it, and two neoclassical pavilions in brick and limestone are placed opposite each other. On the same road is Birr Cross Roads Cemetery, designed by Sir Edwin Lutyens. The town of Zillebeke is the location of several cemeteries and memorials. Tuileries British Cemetery contains the remains of nearly 100 casualties. Bedford House Cemetery was designed by Wilfred Von Berg and is situated in the grounds of the former Chateau Rosendael, which was used by the British as a divisional headquarters. In the grounds of Palingbeek estate, five cemeteries can be found. Spoilbank Cemetery, on the canal, was designed by Sir Edwin Lutyens in collaboration with William Cowlishaw and contains the bodies and remains of 520 casualties. A Cross of

War graves, Ypres Salient.

Sacrifice is placed on the north wall. Less than 200 meters from this graveyard is Chester Farm Cemetery. Chester Farm Cemetery and Woods Cemetery, also in the grounds of Palingbeek, were designed by Lutyens and Cowlishaw. The two other cemeteries in the grounds, First DCLI Cemetery, The Buff, and Hedge Row Trench Cemetery, are smaller cemeteries and were both designed by John Truelove.

South of Zillebeke, near Hill 60, is the Caterpillar Crater, one of the best preserved mine craters of the Ypres Salient. In Hollebeke, a brick memorial displaying a commemorative plaque recalls the first attacks of Indian troops during the First World War. It was unveiled in 1999. Close to the parish church of Hollebeke is a stone memorial and sculpture of a soldier, a Poilu, honouring military and civilian casualties. Wijtschate, a well-known village in the Heuvelland region of the Westhoek, has ten British military cemeteries and several mine craters, remnants of the Battle of Messines Ridge of 1917.

The Canadian Hill 62 Memorial near Ypres. Originally, this location was considered for the Canadian National Memorial. The granite block is one of six identical memorial stones, differentiated by their inscriptions.

Lone Tree Crater near Mesen/Messines, also known as the Pond of Peace, is a remnant of the Battle of Messines. Tangible relics of the war have become places of pilgrimage, becoming places of remembrance.

Left: Memorial Cross of the 16th Irish Division, Wijtschate.

Below: Wytschaete Military Cemetery contains 1,003 Commonwealth burials, of which 674 could not be identified. The cemetery was designed by Sir Edwin Lutyens.

Spanbroekmolen British Cemetery is located near the Lone Tree Crater memorial pond. The Lone Tree Crater, also known as the Spanbroekmolen Mine Crater Memorial, is a remnant of the mines that launched the Battle of Messines on 7 June 1917, in Flemish also known as the Battle of the Mines. Water has filled the basin left by the mine explosion, transforming the crater into a pond, today called the Pool of Peace. Other remnants of the Mines battle are Peckham Crater, Ontario Farm Crater or the four craters in Kruisstraat road, but there are many more around Wijtschate. A memorial in the shape of a Celtic cross is dedicated to actions of the

16th Irish Division in the capture of Wijtschate during the Battle of Messines in 1917. It is located next to the Wytschaete Military Cemetery, holding the remains of over 1,000 British and Commonwealth soldiers, reburied at Wytschaete Cemetery after the war. Of special interest are the two memorial pillars on Oosthoekstraat road, one symbolizing the 36th Ulster Division and the other the 16th Irish Division. This modest double memorial commemorates the first joint action of Protestant and Catholic Irish divisions during the war. The main town in Heuvelland is Kemmel, not far from the strategic Kemmelberg Hill. Pond Farm cemetery is one of many burial grounds in the area. It was first established in 1916. Designed by Charles Holden and William Cowlishaw, a low rubble wall encloses the grounds located in the fields between Wulvergem and Lindenhoek.

Kemmel, part of the Ypres Salient, was captured by the Germans in 1918 during the Spring Offensive and finally recaptured on 31 August 1918. The castle of Kemmel was completely destroyed during the war. 1,135 troops of the Commonwealth are buried at the Kemmel Chateau Military Cemetery, which was designed by Sir Edwin Lutyens. In the garden of Godezonne Farm a small graveyard was first established in 1915 by the Royal Scots and the Middlesex Regiment. After the war, casualties of nearby battlefields were reburied at Godezonne, again designed by William Cowlishaw. A low wall in brick and stone encloses the grounds, which are divided in a lower first and a higher second plot. Some steps positioned against the base of the centrally placed Cross of Sacrifice, a recurrent feature at burial grounds by Holden and Cowlishaw, provide access to the second plot.

Bronze plate showing the movements of the Battle of Messines, Island of Ireland Peace Park, Mesen/Messines.

The 36th Ulster Division, 10th Irish Division and 16th Irish Division represented by three pillars, Island of Ireland Peace Park, Mesen/Messines.

Irish House Cemetery, located in the fields east of Kemmel, is designed in the English vernacular style Cowlishaw applied regularly to the smaller cemeteries. The name of the cemetery derives from a now lost farm that was dubbed Irish House. Suffolk Cemetery, designed by John Truelove, is a smaller graveyard first established by the 2nd Battalion the Suffolk Regiment in 1915. On the western flank of Kemmelberg hill the French ossuary of Kemmelberg is situated, commemorating over 5,200 French soldiers, of which only fifty-seven could be identified. The memorial consists of an obelisk surmounted by a Gallic rooster representing the people of France. Mesen, in the English speaking world better known under its French name Messines, is an ancient place and location of Mesen Abbey, which was completely destroyed during the war. The Messines Ridge Memorial, designed by Charles Holden, commemorates those from the New Zealand Expeditionary Force that fell in or near Mesen who have no known grave. It is located west of Mesen on the N314 towards Wulvergem. To commemorate the actions of Irish soldiers at the Battle of Messines Ridge, the Island of Ireland Peace Park was created. On 11 November 1998 the tower, a traditional design of ancient Irish round tower, was inaugurated by the President of Ireland, Her Majesty the Queen and King Albert II of Belgium. Three pillars in the grounds of the park symbolize the 36th Ulster Division, the 10th Irish Division and the 16th Irish Division, the three divisions from the island of Ireland. The Island of Ireland Peace Park is located on the N365 to Ploegsteert. The no man's land between Messines and Ploegsteert, in English also known as Plugstreet, is probably the location of the famed football match during the Christmas Truce of 1914. A small wooden cross in Saint-Yvon reads: '1914 – The Khaki Chum's Christmas Truce – 1999 – 85 Years – Lest We Forget.' Continuing on the N365, one passes the Ploegsteert Memorial to the Missing, designed by Harold Chalton Bradshaw. The white stone structure on a circular plan is dedicated to the 11,390 missing from several battles outside the Ypres Salient and wider Ploegsteert area. The sculpture is by Gilbert Ledward. The memorial was inaugurated by HRH the Duke of Brabant, the future King Leopold III, in 1931. A Last Post ceremony is heard every first Friday of the month. In the near vicinity of the memorial are several cemeteries. A first cemetery was established in 1915, called Hyde Park Corner (Royal Berks) Cemetery, and extended a year later with the Berks Cemetery Extension. Just south of Ploegsteert Wood is the Strand Military Cemetery, designed by Charles Holden and William Cowlishaw. From Messines road towards the wood a long trench was located, dubbed The Strand, after which the cemetery was named. The Strand cemetery was one of the first British burial places on Belgian soil during the First World War. Already in October 1914, the first casualties were buried here. During the Spring Offensive the site was captured by the Germans. After the war burials from other graveyards from the wider region were relocated to The Strand. Eleven casualties are remembered by a Duhallow Block, a special memorial stone erected by the Commonwealth War Graves Commission to commemorate those whose graves were destroyed in later battles: 'Their Glory Shall Not Be Blotted Out.'

Playing football in No Man's Land, Christmas 1914.

French Flanders
and Artois

Le Grand Hasard Military Cemetery in Morbecque/ Moerbeke, France. A preliminary cemetery was established by the 31st Division in 1918, when the Spring Offensive had pushed the Western Front close to the village of Morbecque in the French Westhoek.

Le Peuplier Military Cemetery, designed by John Truelove.

Le Peuplier Military
Cemetery, Kaaster/
Caëstre, France.

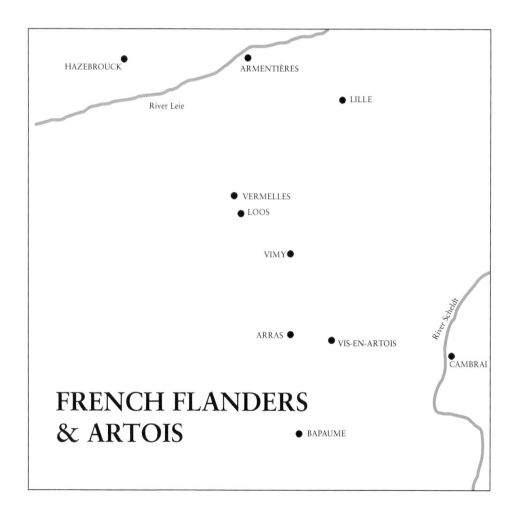

HAZEBROUCK

ARMENTIÈRES

River Leie

LILLE

VERMELLES

LOOS

VIMY

ARRAS

VIS-EN-ARTOIS

River Scheldt

CAMBRAI

FRENCH FLANDERS
& ARTOIS

BAPAUME

Over the centuries the regions of northern France have witnessed the passing of many soldiers and some decisive battles, including the Battle of Hondschoote of 1793. Of strategic importance was the town of Cassel, located on a hill, with a history dating back to at least Roman times. The Flemish history of the Nord-Pas-de-Calais region of northern France can be understood in the names of the towns and villages. During most of the First World War this part of French Flanders was in Allied hands. That changed during the Spring Offensive of 1918 when Hazebrouck came in the frontline. The area around Hazebrouck became part of some attempts to break the frontline. Several military cemeteries in the villages and hamlets around Hazebrouck date of this period. Le Peuplier Military Cemetery at Caëstre/Kaaster was first established in April 1918 during the German Spring Offensive. Designed by William Cowlishaw, the cemetery contains 190 British and Commonwealth burials. This modest graveyard with its brick wall, marked by a limestone Cross of Sacrifice, somewhere in the fields outside a village, is one of many such graveyards in Belgian and French Flanders. Morbecque/Moerbeke, a village south of Hazebrouck, is the location of Le Grand Hasard Military Cemetery, first established in summer 1918. Of the 448 casualties buried at this cemetery, 310 fell during the First World War, the remaining 138 during the Second, in May and June 1940. Placed centrally is a Cross of Sacrifice. The cemetery is typical of the work of Sir Herbert Baker. In the centre of the village is the Morbecque British Cemetery, designed by George H. Goldsmith, established by the 5th Division in April 1918. Again, a Cross of Sacrifice is placed centrally at the entrance of the grounds, which are enclosed by a low stone wall. There are 105 identified burials of the First World War in this cemetery. The town of Armentières is located on the Belgian–French border just south of Ploegsteert. Here, the forty-seven officers and men of the New Zealand Division who fell in action and have no known grave are remembered by the Cité Bonjean Memorial. It is one of four memorials commemorating the missing of the New Zealand Division on the Western Front in France; the other three are at Marfaux, Grévillers and Longueval. South of Armentières, on the D 22 in Bois Grenier, a village that was on the front during most of the war, there are several war cemeteries, of which the Y Farm Military Cemetery is the largest, containing 822 burials. Most of the British and Commonwealth casualties were buried here after the war had ended and were relocated to Y Farm cemetery from burial grounds in the region. The cemetery was designed by Sir Herbert Baker.

On the location of the Battle of Fromelles, an attack on the German defensive line which took place on 19–20 July 1916, a memorial park was created commemorating the actions of the Australian forces. The Battle of Fromelles signified the first action of the Australian Imperial Force at the Western Front. A sculpture dedicated to the

Morbecque British Cemetery,
Moerbeke/Morbecque, France.

La Kreule Military Cemetery,
Hazebrouck, commemorates 588
casualties of the First World War. It was
designed by Sir Herbert Baker.

men who fought and fell during the Battle of Fromelles was commissioned by the Office of Australian War Graves. The sculpture depicts two figures, one soldier carrying another, and was made by Peter Corlett of Melbourne. The Memorial Park was officially opened on 5 July 1998. The VC Corner Australian Cemetery at Fromelles is dedicated to the casualties of the First Australian Imperial Force. These bodies remain unidentified. It was established at the end of the First World War and honours some 410 casualties brought from the surrounding battlefields. In front of the stone and flint wall with two flanking pavilions on the far ends, a Cross of Sacrifice is centrally placed. Both the memorial and cemetery were designed by Sir Herbert Baker. Nearby is the Pheasant Wood Military Cemetery, dedicated in 2010, built after the discovery of mass graves in 2008. The British and Australian governments had asked to construct a new site to house these newly discovered remains. It was designed by Barry Edwards and executed by Betonbouw Bentein BVBA from Langemark, Belgium, a company that among other things renovates military cemeteries. Pheasant Wood Military Cemetery was the first war cemetery built by the Commonwealth War Graves Commission in fifty years.

Gun crews near
Armentières,1916.

Woburn Abbey Cemetery,
Cuinchy, begun by the Royal
Berkshire Regiment in 1915.
The burial grounds were
designed by Charles Holden.

The Aubers Ridge British cemetery, in Aubers, is the final resting place of 720 casualties, of which 442 remain unidentified. It was designed by Charles Holden and William Cowlishaw. The site contains a Cross of Sacrifice and a Stone of Remembrance. The Indian Memorial to the Missing in Neuve-Chapelle, designed by Sir Herbert Baker, honours the 4,742 soldiers of the British Indian Army who gave their lives during the First World War. It is the only Indian war memorial dedicated to the fallen of the First World War. The white stone column, flanked by two tigers, is adorned by representations of the Star of India, the Imperial Crown and a lotus flower. A Stone of Remembrance is placed at the base of the monument. In 2015 the Prime Minister of India, Narendra Modi, visited the memorial. In Laventie, on the way between Armentières and Béthune, several war cemeteries can be found, including the Euston Post Cemetery, the Laventie Military Cemetery and the Royal Irish Rifles Graveyard. The Rue-du-Bacquerot No. 1 Military Cemetery, off the D169 road outside Le Grand Chemin, was designed by Sir Herbert Baker and is the final resting place for 487 British, 144 Indian and German soldiers. Special memorials have been erected at the cemetery to commemorate twelve victims whose graves could not be located.

On the D171 road to Béthune is the Le Touret Memorial. An impressive portico, designed by J. R. Truelove, provides the entrance to an enclosed green with a column engraved with the numerals 1914–1918. The Le Touret Memorial to the Missing honours the nearly 14,000 British men who gave their lives in the region between the Lys and La Bassée between October 1914 and September 1915. On the edge of the cemetery a Cross of Sacrifice is placed. The neoclassical design of the buildings is by Sir Herbert Baker. In Givenchy-lès-la-Bassée, on the Canal de la Deûle east of Béthune, a memorial cross is dedicated to the actions of the 55th West Lancashire Division at Givenchy in April 1918. On the other side of the canal in Cuinchy, Woburn Abbey Cemetery can be found, the final resting place of 315 identified Commonwealth soldiers. A low rubble wall encloses the grounds, designed by Charles Holden, two small pavilions and a cross of sacrifice are placed on the back wall.

The medieval village and castle of Vermelles, like so many towns and villages on the Western Front, were completely destroyed during the First World War. Today, a cemetery can be found on the site of the former castle square. It is one of several military cemeteries in and around Vermelles. The larger, Vermelles British Cemetery, was designed by Sir Herbert Baker and contains 2,145 burials. Just outside the village stands a cross dedicated to the 46th (North Midland) Division. It commemorates the actions of the 46th Division at the Battle of Loos, which took place in autumn 1915. The Battle of Loos was part of a larger British and French attempt in Artois and Champagne to break through the defensive lines and restore a war of movement from the trench warfare. The more than 20,000 British and Commonwealth soldiers who gave their lives during this battle and have no known grave are remembered by the Loos Memorial in Loos-en-Gohelle. The names are

Memorial cross of the 46th (North Midland) Division in Vermelles.

written on walls which enclose Dud Corner Cemetery. The domed pavilions give the enclosed space of the cemetery a distinct impression. Loos Memorial and Dud Corner Cemetery were designed by Sir Herbert Baker and inaugurated in 1930.

Halfway between Béthune and Arras on the D937 is the location of the Notre-Dame-de-Lorette French Military Cemetery and Memorial, the largest French military cemetery with over 40,000 casualties. It is located at Ablain-Saint-Nazaire to the north-west of Arras. A strategic site dominating the Douai plain, the grounds were heavily contested between French and German troops during the three Battles of Artois. The basilica and tower of the Nécropole Nationale were designed by Louis Marie Cordonnier in a neo-Byzantine style. The freestanding tower, or lantern of the dead, is 52 meters high. The present basilica replaces an original chapel dedicated to Our Lady of Loreto erected on this location in 1727. On 11 November 2014 the new memorial Ring of Remembrance, Anneau de la Mémoire, was unveiled on the site, a contemporary addition to the Nécropole Nationale. Designed by French architect Philippe Prost, the ring commemorates 479,606 soldiers from forty nations who gave their lives during the years of the First World War whose names are engraved on 500 gilded plaques. These names are listed alphabetically, without observation of rank or nationality. The Ring of Remembrance was unveiled on 11 November 2014, marking the centennial of the start of the First World War. Two other memorial sites in the municipality of Souchez are of great interest, the Cabaret-Rouge British Cemetery and the Canadian Memorial. The Cabaret-Rouge Cemetery and Memorial, designed in a neoclassical style by the architect Captain Frank Higginson, honours 7,665 fallen Commonwealth soldiers. A building with a stone dome provides entrance to one of the largest Commonwealth cemeteries in the region.

The Church of Notre Dame de Lorette, designed by Louis-Marie Cordonnier, in the grounds of the French National War Cemetery in Ablain-Saint-Nazaire.

The Cabaret-Rouge British Cemetery near Souchez was designed by Frank Higginson, a captain in the Canadian Army during the First World War, in 1926.

Headstones at Cabaret-Rouge British Cemetery.

THE LAND ON WHICH THIS CEMETERY STANDS IS THE FREE GIFT OF THE FRENCH PEOPLE FOR THE PERPETUAL RESTING PLACE OF THOSE OF THE ALLIED ARMIES WHO FELL IN THE WAR OF 1914-1918 AND ARE HONOURED HERE

Commemorative plaque, Cabaret-Rouge British Cemetery.

The Second Battle of Arras, 9 April to 16 May 1917, was the longest advance by the British since the beginning of the trench warfare on the Western Front. Part of the offensive is known as the Battle of Vimy Ridge, which resulted in the capture of the ridge between Arras and Lens. The attack of Vimy Ridge was meticulously planned by General Byng and was the first joint attack of all four Canadian divisions. Part of this former battlefield has become the Canadian National Vimy Memorial. Designed and made by the Canadian sculptor Walter Seymour Allward, the monument stands on top of a hill, named Hill 145 during the war and the highest point of Vimy Ridge. Centrally placed are two 30-meter-tall pylons, one featuring the maple representing Canada and the other the fleur-de-lys representing France. On the outer wall the names of 11,285 casualties are inscribed. The statue, popularly known as Mother Canada, is symbolic for what the Vimy Memorial represents today, the location where the nation of Canada mourns her dead fallen on the Western Front. The Vimy Memorial has become the Canadian symbol and a place of pilgrimage. The Memorial was unveiled by King Edward VIII and French President Lebrun in 1936.

Outside Thélus, south of Vimy, the Canadian Corps Artillery Memorial honours the men of the Canadian Corps Artillery who gave their lives during the Vimy battles in 1917. In the fields outside Thélus there are some interesting Commonwealth cemeteries to be found. Zivy Crater (CB1 Cemetery) off the D49 between Thélus and Neuville-St-Vaast is an enwalled mine crater and mass grave. It was designed by William

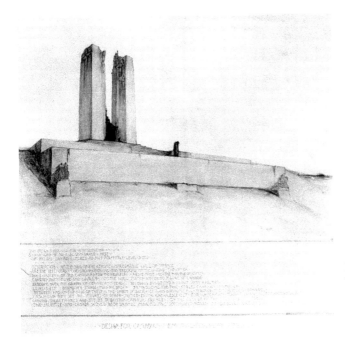

Design submission by Walter Allward for the Canadian National Memorial, finally built in Vimy, France.

Representing France and Canada, the two pylons of the Canadian Memorial symbolise the unity and sacrifice of both nations.

Cowlishaw in a free composition and has no headstones; instead, the names of the fifty-three casualties are engraved on plaques. A Cross of Sacrifice stands on the edge of the crater, to the right of the entrance. A few hundred meters south of Zivy Crater is the somewhat larger Lichfield Crater (CB2 Cemetery). The concept is similar: a large enwalled crater without individual headstones for the fallen soldiers, whose names are engraved on three stone plaques. A commanding Cross of Sacrifice overlooks the empty green of Lichfield Crater. Both are typical of the vernacular by William Cowlishaw. In the centre of Thélus there is a memorial dedicated to the Canadian artillery. In front of the town hall is the French memorial, a classic Poilu figure on a pedestal with plaques engraved with the names of local victims of the First World War.

Taking the D49 towards Bailleul-Sir-Berthoult, just on the edge of Thélus is the Bois Carré British Cemetery. A simple cross in the fields to the right of the D49 is dedicated to the actions of the 1st Canadian Division. In the village of Gavrelle is a memorial to the 63rd Royal Naval Division, a large anchor placed inside a ruined red brick building. Memorial plaques are placed on the outer wall. The highly original memorial was unveiled on 8 May 1991. The Point du Jour Cemetery is on the D950 road to Arras. Designed by Sir Reginald Blomfield, the cemetery is the final resting place of 803 casualties, of which 401 remain unidentified. In the near vicinity the 9th Scottish Division Memorial can be found. It commemorates the actions of the 9th Scottish Division during the Battle of Arras on 9 April 1917. For visitor safety reasons the memorial, consisting of a tower of boulders, was moved to its present location near the Point du Jour British Cemetery.

Arras, medieval cathedral city and ancient capital of Artois, was largely destroyed during the war. The reconstructed belfry, like its counterpart in Ypres, is a symbol of resilience and the rebuilding of the city after the war. A monument dedicated to

Above: Names on the walls of the Canadian National Memorial.

Left: Monument to the victims of the First World War at Neuville-Saint-Vaast.

The Monument to the War
Victims of Arras is one of
the best known works of the
French artist F. A. Desruelles.

the victims of the First World War is located in Foch Square opposite the railway
station. The memorial was unveiled in 1931 and renovated in 2007. It was made
by Félix-Alexandre Desruelles after winning a competition. It consists of a column
and an angel representing peace. Just outside Arras, on the Boulevard General De
Gaulle, is the Faubourg d'Amiens British cemetery, designed by Sir Edwin Lutyens.
It is also the location of the Arras Memorial to the Missing, a neoclassical building,
dedicated to the over 34,000 British and Commonwealth casualties with no known
grave who gave their lives on the Western Front in the Arras sector between spring
1916 and early August 1918. The memorial consists of a portico or cloisters, as they
are referred to on Lutyens's plans, a Cross of Sacrifice and Stone of Remembrance.
At Arras, Lutyens shows his interest in English baroque architecture. The works of
Vanbrugh in particular appear to have been the inspiration for this memorial. The
Air Services Memorial, made by the sculptor Sir William Reid Dick, featuring a
globe, was unveiled by Lord Trenchard, Marshal of the Royal Air Force, in 1932. The
obelisk is inscribed with nearly 1,000 names of casualties, men who have no know
graves. On top of the monument is a globe showing the world as it appeared on the
morning of 11 November 1918, the day of armistice. Both Arras war memorials
were inaugurated by Lord Trenchard in 1932. In the southern suburbs of Arras
on the D917 is Beaurains Road Cemetery, by Lutyens. In the street corner of the
grounds is a Cross of Sacrifice, marking the burial grounds. Just outside Arras, on
the D3 towards Foncquevillers, is the Agny Military Cemetery, designed by Lutyens
with William Cowlishaw as assistant architect. Hidden from sight, located in a
residential area, it can be accessed by a path. There are 413 dead commemorated, of
which 118 remain unidentified. The Cross of Sacrifice is placed centrally against the
south-eastern wall of the rectangular grounds.

The Cross of Sacrifice at the
Arras Flying Services Memorial.

The Artois region is the site of many smaller war cemeteries. Of interest is the Ayette Indian and Chinese Cemetery in Ayette, on the D919 to Amiens, the final resting place of men of the Indian and Chinese Labour Corps. In total, 2,000 Chinese and 1,500 Indian labourers lost their lives during the years of the First World War on the Western Front. Some noteworthy memorials are located on or near the D939 road from Arras to Cambrai. The Windmill British Cemetery in Monchy-le-Preux was first established in 1917 to bury the victims of the Second Battle of the Scarpe. It was designed by Sir Edwin Lutyens. In the centre of the village one of five Caribou memorials on the Western Front can be found. It commemorates the actions of the Newfoundland Regiment in the region, more specifically during the Battle of Arras in 1917. On the D939 in Haucourt is the Vis-en-Artois Cemetery and Memorial, designed by J. R. Truelove. Unveiled in 1930, the cemetery is the final resting place of over 2,300 British and Commonwealth soldiers. The memorial is designed in a neoclassical style with columned porticos and two structures inspired by obelisks. Dury on the D939 is the location of the Dury Australian memorial, comprising a small park and a granite block commemorating the actions of the Canadian Expeditionary Force. Similar blocks can be found in Passendale in Belgium and in

Courcelette in France. In the centre of the village is the French Monument to the Dead, a classic Poilu figure on a stand. Dury is also the location of the Dury Mill British Cemetery. Along the Canal du Nord are several cemeteries, testimonies to the heavy clashes that took place to capture this vital and strategic waterway and break through the Hindenburg Line. The Quarry Cemetery in Marquion is a very nicely designed small graveyard. Due to its situation, the cemetery is accessed by some descending stairs. The Cross of Sacrifice is placed higher, at the far end of the rectangular plot. The final resting place of sixty-eight British and Canadian soldiers, the grounds were designed by Sir Edwin Lutyens. The Battle of Havrincourt, which took place on 12 September 1918, is one of the combats piercing the Hindenburg Line. There are several memorials and cemeteries in and around Havrincourt. A classic obelisk was erected to commemorate the actions of the 62nd West Riding Division. The Anneux British Cemetery on the D630 from Cambrai to Bapaume is the final resting place of 1,103 casualties, of which 459 remain unidentified. It was designed by Sir Edwin Lutyens with George Goldsmith as assistant architect. The grounds are accessible by an entrance building in the form of a loggia with Tuscan order columns. The cemetery is architecturally structured by two green ways, one starting from the entrance pavilion, the other connecting a Cross of Sacrifice on one end, the Stone of Remembrance on the other far end of the grounds.

The Cambrai Memorial to the Missing, situated on the D930 Cambrai to Bapaume in Louverval, was designed by Harold Chalton Bradshaw, who also designed the Ploegsteert Memorial, and was unveiled on 4 August 1930. It commemorates those who gave their lives during the Battle of Cambrai in 1917 and have no known grave. The town of Bapaume, dating back to Roman times, was considered to be of strategic significance in the framework of the Somme battles. The town was captured by the Germans in 1914, taken by the British on 17 March 1917 and recaptured by the Germans during the Spring Offensive of 1918. On 29 August 1918 the New Zealand Division was able to liberate Bapaume. There are several memorials and cemeteries in and around Bapaume: Beaulencourt British Cemetery in Ligny-Thilloy, Manchester Cemetery in Riencourt-les-Bapaume and Favreuil British Cemetery, to mention but a few. East of Bapaume is Bancourt British Cemetery, designed by Lutyens, containing 2,480 burials. There are two brick and stone entrance pavilions in an English Palladian style flanking the centrally placed Stone of Remembrance. At the far end of the grounds, and opposite the Stone, is a Cross of Sacrifice.

The landscape between Bapaume and Albert, connected by the D929 road, is highly associated with the Battle of the Somme and the location of some of the most notable memorials of the Western Front.

Left: A headstone at Anneux British Cemetery, established by the 57th Division in 1918.

Below: A view of the Canadian National Vimy Memorial.

THE BATTLEFIELDS OF THE SOMME

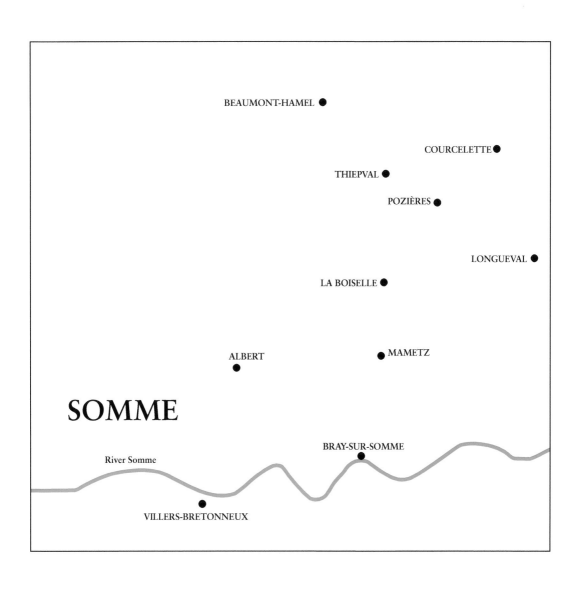

A cemetery near Thiepval.

The Newfoundland Memorial Park in Beaumont Hamel encompasses the largest area of preserved battlegrounds from the Battle of the Somme. It is dedicated to the Royal Newfoundland Regiment but honours all men of the many regiments of the British, French and German armies who fought and died on the Somme battlefields from September 1914 into 1918. Several memorials and cemeteries can be found in the grounds of the park, which was acquired by the people of Newfoundland in 1912. The Caribou Memorial is one of five such dedicatory images made by Basil Gotto commemorating locations on the Western Front where the 1st Battalion Newfoundland Regiment was active. Others can be found in Monchy-le-Preux, Masnieres, Geudecourt in France, and in Harelbeke in Belgium. In the grounds of the Memorial Park the remains of trenches can be found. There are three cemeteries in the grounds, Hawthorn Ridge Cemetery, Hunter's Cemetery and Y Ravine Cemetery. The largest of these is Y Ravine Cemetery; established in 1917, it has 419 burials and commemorates fifty-three soldiers from the United Kingdom and eight from Newfoundland. Hawthorn Ridge Cemetery No. 2 was established in 1917 and has 214 burials. Hunter's Cemetery is a modest circular cemetery of forty-six burials grouped around a Cross of Sacrifice. A bronze sculpture of a Scottish soldier wearing a kilt commemorates the capture of Beaumont-Hamel on 13 November 1916 by the 51st Highland Division. It was made by George Harry Paulin. Close to the entrance, a memorial site is located dedicated to the 29th Division. The 29th Division was formed in 1915 and first sent to Egypt before it was moved to the Western Front in January 1916. The memorial consists of a pyramid-shaped stone with a bronze plaque showing the red triangle divisional badge. Of interest are the remnants of the battlegrounds which determine the atmosphere of the place. There are the remains of several trenches and a replica of the original Danger Tree, at that time located in No Man's Land and used as a landmark during the Battle of the Somme, which contribute to the popularity of the memorial park as a destination for visitors.

The Cimetiere National de Serre-Hébuterne is the final resting place of over 800 French troops who gave their lives in battle between 10 and 13 June 1915 at Hébuterne. The military cemetery is characterised by its white crosses and red roses. It was created between 1919 and 1923 and is looked after by the French War Graves Agency. Also on the D919 is the Serre Road No. 2 Cemetery, designed by Lutyens. It was first established in 1917 and completed in 1934. At the end of the green way stands a Cross of Sacrifice, flanked by two pavilions. A neoclassical gateway building provides the entrance to the grounds. The cemetery is the final resting place of over 7,000 British and Commonwealth troops, of which over 2,100 remain unidentified. To the north-west of Serre the Sheffield Memorial Park is located. The park is dedicated to the memory of the men of the 31st Division and the Pals Battalions. Parts of the grounds are left uneven, revealing the disfigured landscape due to artillery shelling. A red brick memorial is located on the south-east side of the wood and is dedicated to all members of the Accrington Pals who gave their lives in this location during the Battle of the Somme. In the near vicinity of the Memorial Park are several cemeteries. Luke Copse British Cemetery, Puisieux,

The Cross of Sacrifice of Y Ravine
Cemetery, Beaumont-Hamel.

Beaumont-Hamel in 1918.

The Newfoundland
Memorial Park in
Beaumont-Hamel. The
grounds are the largest area
of preserved battlefields
on the Somme, attracting
an increasing number of
visitors to this already
popular site.

The Danger Tree in
the grounds of the
Newfoundland Memorial
Park in Beaumont-Hamel.

contains the bodies and remains of seventy-two casualties, of which twenty-eight remain unidentified. A Cross of Sacrifice is placed near the north-eastern wall. Queens Cemetery in Puisieux holds the graves of 311 soldiers of the First World War. Both cemeteries were designed by N. A. Rew. Railway Hollow Cemetery is the final resting place of sixty-three Commonwealth soldiers who gave their lives on the Somme battlefields. It was designed by Wilfred Von Berg.

Commanding the region north of Albert is an impressive memorial, a masterpiece of British architecture, which for many encompasses the ultimate monument to the victims of the First World War. The Thiepval Memorial to the Missing honours over 72,000 officers and men of the United Kingdom and South Africa who gave their lives on the Somme battlefields before 20 March 1918 and have no known grave. At the foot of the arch the Thiepval Anglo-French Cemetery is located, a cemetery with equal numbers of French and Commonwealth casualties, representing the shared efforts and sacrifice of both nations during the First World War. The memorial, a vast arch built of red brick and limestone, is located on a high ridge and visible for miles around. The names of the fallen are engraved on stone plates placed within

The Anglo-French cemetery in front of the Thiepval Memorial.

A powerful composition placed in an emotionally loaded location: the Thiepval Memorial to the Missing of the Somme.

the monument and a Stone of Remembrance is positioned centrally under the main arch. The Memorial was unveiled in 1932 by Prince Edward, the Prince of Wales, in the presence of the French President, Albert Lebrun. The Thiepval Memorial to the Missing is a monumental structure, standing 43 meters (140 feet) tall. Dominating its surroundings, the building is visible for miles around. The arch, which shows some remarkable similarities to his unexecuted design for Liverpool Cathedral, was designed by Sir Edwin Lutyens in the 1920s and is among his best known structures. The monumentality of Thiepval is very different from the landscape of remembrance that is the memorial park at Beaumont Hamel. They are very different types of memorials, functioning in a different way and created for different purposes. Lutyens designed the perfect setting for official commemorations. The Armistice is commemorated annually by a major ceremony and the start of the Battle of the Somme is observed each year on 1 July. The centennial observance in 2016 was attended by members of the British Royal Family, the Prince of Wales, the Duke and Duchess of Cambridge and Prince Harry. Around 10,000 attended the British National Event that day.

The Ulster Tower Memorial.

The Ulster Tower, the national war memorial of Northern Ireland, officially opened in 1921.

Close to the Thiepval Memorial, on the edge of Thrones Wood, is an obelisk dedicated to those of the 18th Eastern Division who fell in action. Northern Ireland's national war memorial is in the close vicinity on the D73. This memorial was one of the first to be erected on the Western Front and is a close copy of a tower in County Down, Northern Ireland. Many of the men of the 36th Ulster Division were trained at Clandeboye Estate, where the original tower that became the model for this memorial can be found. It was officially opened in 1921. On the edge of Thiepval Wood on the D73 and near the Ulster Tower, Connaught Cemetery can be found. It was designed by Blomfield.

Lochnagar Crater in Ovillers-la-Boisselle is the largest man-made crater on the Western Front and a relic of the Battle of the Somme. Part of the British offensive against the Germans, a mine was detonated underneath a German strongpoint only minutes before the launch of the attack on the morning of 1 July 1916. The remains of the crater developed into a memorial site, attracting visitors from various backgrounds. In 1986 a wooden cross was erected, made from beams of a redundant church near Durham, honouring the many soldiers involved in the attack from the 102nd Tyneside Scottish Brigade and the 103rd Tyneside Irish Brigade.

The area between Albert and Bapaume is the site of several memorials to the Somme battlefields. The Tank Corps Memorial in Pozières commemorates the first usage of tanks in the First World War by the British forces, on 15 September 1916. Australian Memorial Pozières Windmill, and the Tank Corps Memorial on the opposite side of the road, are located on the high northern edge of Pozières, an ideal place of observation. The location of this high ground, which to this day offers views of the surrounding countryside, had been the objective of a British offensive in summer 1916. Pozières was captured by the 1st Australian Division in July 1916, and soon

Lochnagar Mine Crater,
Ovillers-la-Boisselle.

The entrance building, designed by William Cowlishaw, to the Pozières British Cemetery and Memorial is of a classical beauty.

Pozières British Cemetery and Memorial.

Obelisk dedicated to the 1st Australian Division, near Pozières.

afterwards a memorial site was established at the location, commemorating those of the 1st Australian Division who gave their lives on the Western Front in 1916, 1917 and 1918. Similar obelisks with bronze plaques were erected to commemorate those of the 3rd and 4th Australian Divisions. The village of Pozières is the site of the battle of the same name. Several cemeteries and memorials can be found in and around the village. The Pozières Memorial to the Missing commemorates 14,655 British and 300 South Africans who gave their lives on the Somme battlefields between 21 March 1918 and 7 August 1918. The names of the missing casualties are inscribed on ninety-seven panels surrounding the Pozières British Cemetery. A monumental arch designed in a neoclassical style gives entrance to the enclosed cemetery. The words, 'In Memory of the Officers and Men of the Fifth and Fourth Armies who fought on the Somme Battlefields 21st March – 7th August 1918 and of those of their dead who have no known Graves,' are inscribed above the entrance. On the far end of the green way a Cross of Sacrifice is positioned. The Cemetery and Memorial were designed by William Cowlishaw and unveiled in 1930.

Courcelette, on the crossroads of the D929 and D107, was the site of the Battle of Flers-Courcelette during the Somme Offensive of 1916. The village, like so many on the Western Front, was razed to the ground. A grey granite monument south of Courcelette on the D929 commemorates the actions of the Canadian Corps during the Somme Offensive. It is one of a series of similar blocks of remembrance; others can be found at Passendale, Hill 62 or Bourlon Wood.

Longueval is the location of the only memorial commemorating the South African forces in the First World War. The memorial, designed by Sir Herbert Baker, consists of an archway and semi-circular stone wall. The domed arch is surmounted by a bronze sculpture of a horse and two men, representing the British and the Afrikaans peoples

'The Canadian Corps Bore a Valiant Part in Forcing Back the Germans on These Slopes During the Battles of the Somme Sept. 3rd – Nov. 18th 1916.' The Canadian Memorial at Courcelette.

Delville Wood Cemetery with, in
the background, the South African
National Memorial, designed by
Sir Herbert Baker.

of South Africa. In the near vicinity of the memorial is Delville Wood Cemetery, one
of the largest British and Commonwealth cemeteries of the Somme battlefields. It is
the final resting place of over 5,500 casualties of British and Commonwealth forces,
of which more than 3,500 bodies remain unidentified. The cemetery was created
after the Armistice and contains the relocated remains of casualties from various
cemeteries and battlefield burial sites in the region, who fell during the Battle of the
Somme. Two neoclassical pavilions, a Stone of Remembrance and a Cross of Sacrifice
at the end of a green way are part of the landscaping of the grounds. The South
Africa Memorial, Delville Wood, is the only national memorial honouring all South
Africans who participated on the Western Front. Sir Herbert Baker, the architect, had
worked in South Africa for many years, designing the Union Buildings in Pretoria
and St George's Cathedral in Cape Town. The memorial stands at the culmination
of a central green avenue leading into Delville Wood. The unveiling of the memorial
took place on 10 October 1926, attended by Field Marshal Douglas Haig and Prince
Arthur of Connaught, who had been Governor-General of the Union of South Africa
in the preceding years. Surrounding the village of Longueval are several cemeteries
and some memorials worth mentioning. A simple wooden cross just outside the village
commemorates the casualties of the 12th Battalion the Gloucestershire Regiment
who died in the battles of 1916. London Cemetery and Extension is the largest
British military cemetery of the Somme battlefields, containing over 3,800 bodies,
of which 3,114 remain unidentified. The grounds, designed by Sir Herbert Baker,
include a Cross of Sacrifice and a Stone of Remembrance. A brick pavilion provides
entrance to the grounds. Caterpillar Valley Cemetery contains the bodies and
remains of over 5,500 Commonwealth casualties. The Caterpillar Valley Memorial is
dedicated to the over 1,200 officers and men of the New Zealand Division who gave
their lives during the Somme Offensive. It is one of seven memorials on the Western

Front dedicated to those of the New Zealand Division. Other cemeteries include Thistle Dump Cemetery and Longueval Road Cemetery. Péronne Road Cemetery is located at Maricourt on the D938 road from Péronne to Albert. Maricourt was a meeting point between British and French troops at the beginning of the Somme battles in 1916. During the Spring Offensive the village was taken by the Germans, but would be recaptured in August 1918. Péronne Road Cemetery was designed by Sir Herbert Baker.

Right: The Cross of Sacrifice, Péronne Road Cemetery, Maricourt.

Below: Péronne Road Cemetery near Maricourt.

The village of Mametz, a few miles to the west of Albert, was captured by the British on 1 July 1916, the first day of the Somme Offensive. Devonshire Cemetery is the burial site of those of the 8th and 9th Battalions of the Devonshire Regiment who fell in action during that event, including the war poet William Noel Hodgson. In the near vicinity is Gordon Cemetery, designed by Arthur Hutton, the burial place of those of the 2nd Gordon Highlanders who fell during the first day of the Somme Offensive. The village of Mametz was completely destroyed, like so many on the Western Front, and later received a War Cross, a French military decoration. Outside the village, in a hilly field, stands a red dragon, symbolising Wales, on a 3-meter-tall stone plinth. The memorial commemorates the 38th Division's attack on Mametz Wood between 7 and 14 July 1916. Made by Welshman David Petersen and commissioned by the South Wales Branch of the Western Front Association, the memorial was unveiled in 1987. Just north of Fricourt is a German military cemetery, the last resting place of German troops who lost their lives on the Somme battlefields between September 1914 and 1918. A field of crosses represents more than 17,000 soldiers who lost their lives. The cemetery was started in 1920 by relocating bodies of German war casualties to Fricourt and was completed in its present form in 1977. Like other German military cemeteries, it is in the care of the Volksbund Deutsche Gräberfürsorge e.V., the German War Graves Agency.

Between Maricourt and Bray is the Bronfay Farm Military Cemetery, first established in 1914 by French troops and used during the Somme battles by the British. The grounds, containing 537 burials, can be accessed by a simple brick entrance pavilion. Bronfay Farm Military cemetery was designed by Sir Edwin Lutyens with George Goldsmith as assistant architect.

Bray on the River Somme was initially captured by the Imperial German Troops in 1914, yet was soon retaken by the French. The Spring Offensive of 1918 brought the town back into the front line. In the town centre a granite monument is dedicated to the victims of the war from the community. It was unveiled in 1924. The French military cemetery of Bray, on the D329 road to Albert, contains the bodies of over 1,000 soldiers. Many of them gave their lives during the Battle of the Somme in 1916. White crosses represent the war casualties. Outside the town, the Bray Vale British Cemetery contains 279 burials from the First World War. Bray Hill British Cemetery, on the D329 road to Albert, contains 105 burials from the First World War. A low brick wall encloses a rectangular graveyard; a Cross of Sacrifice stands at the far end of the cemetery, flanked by two trees. Both burial grounds were designed by Arthur Hutton. In the centre of Chipilly, a hamlet on the River Somme, a memorial made by the French sculptor Henri Gauquié, honours those of the 58th London Division who fell during the Battle of Amiens in August 1918. The design is untypical, representing

Devonshire Cemetery, designed by William Cowlishaw, near Mametz. Devonshire Cemetery is the final resting place of the war poet William Noel Hodgson.

General view of the Somme battlefield.

an artilleryman cradling the head of a horse, and honours the many thousands wounded and dead war horses of all sides. The wounded horse monument is located near the church and was inaugurated in 1922. On the other side of the River Somme is the town of Le Hamel, the location of a successful attack by Australian and US armies, on 4 July 1918. The site of the Battle of Hamel, the first attack planned and carried out by the commander of the Australian Corps, General Sir John Monash, is the location of the Australian Corps Memorial Park. It is dedicated to the over 100,000 of the Australian Corps who served in France during the years of the First World War. On the eightieth anniversary of the Battle of Hamel the lands on which the memorial park is situated were given to the Australian people. The monument consists of three blocks of curved granite; the central block features the bronze badge of the Australian forces. On the D23 between Corbie and Villers Bretonneux, the Australian National Memorial can be found. This is where in 1918 the German advances toward Amiens were halted by the Australian divisions. The memorial is dedicated to all of the Australian soldiers who fought on the Western Front during the First World War. It was unveiled by King George VI in 1938.

The Villers-Bretonneux Military Cemetery has two large neoclassical pavilions and a Stone of Remembrance at the entrance of the grounds. A tower, providing views of the surrounding Somme battlefields, forms the central part of the memorial and the visual culmination of the cemetery. It forms the background for commemorations such as the recent Anzac (Australian and New Zealand Army Corps) Day observance, on 25 April 2018, attended by HRH the Prince of Wales. The Memorial and Cemetery were designed by Sir Edwin Lutyens in the British neoclassical tradition. Created after the end of the war, the cemetery contains the remains of over 2,100 Commonwealth troops, bodies and remains from several burial sites and battlefields in the region.

The Australian War Memorial and Cemetery at Villers-Bretonneux.

AISNE: THE LONG ROAD TO COMPIÈGNE

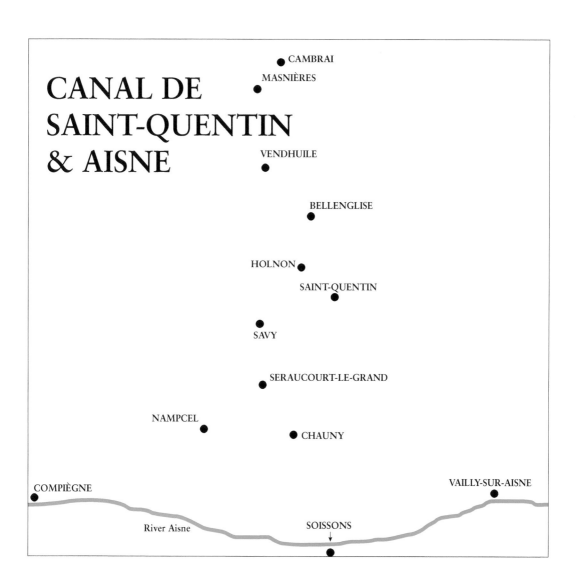

CAMBRAI

MASNIÈRES

**CANAL DE
SAINT-QUENTIN
& AISNE**

VENDHUILE

BELLENGLISE

HOLNON

SAINT-QUENTIN

SAVY

SERAUCOURT-LE-GRAND

NAMPCEL

CHAUNY

COMPIÈGNE

VAILLY-SUR-AISNE

River Aisne

SOISSONS

Unicorn Cemetery, Vendhuile, designed by Charles Holden.

In late autumn 1917, the first Battle of Cambrai took place. Breaking the Hindenburg Line and capturing the Saint-Quentin Canal, which was part of the German defensive line, was the objective. An initial success, partly due to the actions of British tanks, the attack was countered by the German troops the following day; however, the vital lesson of Cambrai was that even the strongest trenches, the Hindenburg Line, could be overcome. Innovative material and tactics were crucial. The Royal Tank Regiment remember the battle and their actions annually on Cambrai Day. Commemorating the actions of the Royal Newfoundland Regiment is the typical caribou memorial on the D644 from Cambrai to Masnières. The monument is placed in a small park. It is one of five identical memorials on the Western Front; others are found in Beaumont Hamel, Monchy-le-Preux, Guedecourt and Courtrai/Kortrijk. A sixth bronze caribou can be found in Bowring Park, St John's, Newfoundland, Canada. On the road to Marcoing is Masnieres British Cemetery, established in September 1918 as a burial site for troops fallen during the first Battle of Cambrai. The cemetery is the final resting place of 225 soldiers, of which 147 are British, fifty-nine are German and nineteen are from New Zealand. The grounds were designed by Charles Holden. Near the village of Vendhuile on the D28 is the Unicorn Cemetery. The name derives from the 50th (Northumbrian) Division emblem.

It is in the close vicinity of the Autoroute des Anglais. An initial attempt to capture the village during the Battle of Cambrai failed; Vendhuile was finally taken in September 1918. Designed by Charles Holden, Unicorn Cemetery contains the remains and bodies of 1,008 casualties, of which 409 remain unidentified. These remains were relocated from other smaller burial places in the region, such as La Paurelle Cemetery in Ronssoy and Lempire British Cemetery in Lempire. A Duhallow Block remembers eight casualties originally buried at Lempire.

Above left: The Newfoundland Memorial in Masnières is one of five similar caribou monuments on the Western Front.

Above right: La Baraque British Cemetery, near Bellenglise, contains sixty-two burials. The cemetery was designed by Charles Holden.

On the D 57 between Bony and Hargicourt is the Somme American Cemetery and Memorial. The grounds contain over 1,800 graves of US soldiers who lost their lives during the Battle of Saint-Quentin Canal in late 1918. It was designed by George Howe and Marcel Loyau and dedicated in 1937.

The grounds have a rectangular shape and are lined with trees. Two stone pathways divide the grounds into four sectors containing white crosses. A flagpole is positioned in the crossing of the two paths. In the grounds of the cemetery is a chapel with a bronze door; the names of the 333 missing are engraved on the walls. The Hargicourt Communal Cemetery Extension is situated just outside the village, close to the D572. In 1917 the village of Hargicourt was taken by British troops but it was recaptured by the Germans during the Spring Offensive of 1918. Originally, the grounds were located beyond the German military burial grounds of the local Protestant Communal Cemetery; today, the extension is located separately after the German graves were relocated. To the west of the village, south of the D406 towards Péronne, is the Hargicourt British War Memorial and Cemetery. Over 300 casualties from the First World War are commemorated here. In Bellicourt on the D331 is the Bellicourt British cemetery. Designed by Charles Holden, the grounds contain over 1,200 burials of the First World War. A semi-circular wall is placed at the far end of the grounds, forming the background for a semi-circular stone bench. The Cross of Sacrifice is placed in a corner on the road side of the grounds, marking the location of these British burial grounds.

On the D1044 road between Bellicourt and Le Catelet is Bellicourt American Monument, a white stone memorial dedicated to the 90,000 American troops who served in France with the British during the last years of the First World War. It was

Above left: Joncourt British Cemetery.

Above right: Joncourt East British Cemetery.

designed by the Franco-American architect Paul Philip Cret, who also designed the Flanders Field American Cemetery and Memorial in Waregem, Belgium. The impressive white block recalls the Stone of Remembrance by Lutyens in design. A map of the battlegrounds is engraved on the back of the monument. A few miles south of Bellicourt is the hamlet of Bellenglise. Bellenglise had been in German hands for most of the war. In September 1918 the 46th (North Midland) Division was able to capture the village. The La Baraque British Cemetery is located just to the north of Bellenglise, on the road to Saint-Quentin. It was established in 1918. The composition is put together freely. The Cross of Sacrifice is placed at the entrance and steps on one side of the memorial give access to the burial grounds, which are enclosed by a low rubble wall. The cemetery contains the remains of sixty-two soldiers. In the fields between Bellenglise and Joncourt, on the N44, is the Joncourt British Cemetery. East of the hamlet of Joncourt is Joncourt East British Cemetery. Both cemeteries were designed by William Cowlishaw. The nearby village of Ramicourt was captured by the British on 3 October 1918 and a cemetery to bury the casualties was established immediately afterwards. The Ramicourt British Cemetery, designed by William Cowlishaw, is the final resting place of 118 casualties of the First World War. The hamlet of Sequehart on the D31 is the location of two smaller war cemeteries. Sequehart British Cemetery No. 1 was established by the 1st/6th Sherwood Foresters in 1918. It contains fifty-six bodies of soldiers who all fell in the first eight days of October that year. Sequehart British Cemetery No. 2 is in the close vicinity; it contains the bodies of sixty-two casualties of the First World War. A seemingly bucolic farmland, bloodstained, the Crosses of Sacrifice mark these locations as the sites where the war casualties gave their lives, transforming the countryside into a landscape of memories.

The city of Saint-Quentin was founded by the Romans and is located in a strategic location on the River Somme. Already during the Franco-Prussian War the city had been on the front line, suffering many losses on both sides. The First World War proved to be a heavy burden for the ancient town. Captured in August 1914 by the Germans, Saint-Quentin became part of the Hindenburg Line in 1916. Most of the historic town centre, including the impressive medieval basilica, was heavily damaged. A large monument located in a park very near the place where the Saint-Quentin Canal meets the River Somme was erected in commemoration. Designed by Paul Bigot, it is dedicated to the victims of the First World War, the Franco-Prussian War of 1870–71 and the battles of 1557. The structure, showing Bigot's keen interest in Roman architecture, is 31 meters long and 8 meters tall and was inaugurated in 1927. The names of 1,361 war victims, soldiers and casualties of the occupation, are engraved on the columns.

In the centre of Saint-Quentin is a monument honouring King-Soldier Albert of Belgium. It was made by Ernest Diosi and unveiled in 1936. In his inauguration speech, the mayor of St-Quentin describes King Albert as the personification of honour, loyalty and chivalry. There are several military cemeteries in and around Saint-Quentin. Worth mentioning are the French Nécropole Nationale and the German Military Cemetery. The latter was first established in 1914 and originally contained the remains of German, French and German soldiers. A memorial partially in the form of an ancient Greek temple was established in 1915 and officially unveiled by Emperor Wilhelm II. Two bronze statues of ancient warriors are placed in front of an ornate wall. The monument was designed in the neo-baroque Wilhelmine style. After the end of the Second World War the grounds were redesigned and given the typical crosses that can be found in many German military cemeteries in France.

On the D1029 road to Amiens is the French National Cemetery, or Nécropole Nationale de Saint-Quentin. It was founded in 1923 and extended between 1934 and 1935. The vast grounds contain the remains of over 5,000 casualties, relocated from smaller burial grounds in the Aisne region. Nearly 4,000 individual graves are mostly marked by crosses.

West of Saint-Quentin, also on the D1029 road, is the village of Holnon. Located in a residential area of the town is the Chapelle British Cemetery. The name recalls a chapel in this spot destroyed during the war. Established in 1918, there are over 600 burials, mostly relocated from preliminary burial sites in the area, in this cemetery. To the south of Holnon is Savy, where Savy British Cemetery can be found. It was established in 1919. The prominent position of the Stone of Sacrifice, elevated and on the road side of the cemetery, marks this site as the location of British tombs. This location emphasizes the connotation of the Stone as a cenotaph.

Saint-Quentin Monument to the victims of the war. The granite monument, unveiled in 1927, is 31 meters long and 8 meters tall. The names of the victims are engraved on the columns and the friezes are dedicated to the casualties of the war of 1557 and the Franco-Prussian War of 1870–1.

King Albert Memorial, Saint-Quentin. During the war, the person of King-Soldier Albert I of Belgium was highly esteemed in France.

French National Cemetery at Saint-Quentin.

Beeches with distinct burgundy coloured leaves surround the burial grounds. A low rubble wall encloses the grounds, which contain the remains of 868 casualties. Savy British Cemetery was designed by Charles Holden.

On the River Somme lies the village of Seraucourt-le-Grand. During the Spring Offensive the Germans were able to take this village from the Fifth Army. Between 1920 and 1926 Grand-Seraucourt British Cemetery was created, containing the remains of 1,340 British and Commonwealth soldiers, of which 844 remain unidentified. There are two Duhallow Blocks in the grounds commemorating thirty-two casualties whose graves were previously located in German military cemeteries. Grand Seraucourt British Cemetery was designed by Charles Holden and William Cowlishaw. The road side of the grounds, displaying a convincing composition of masses, is typical of the restrained classicism of Holden.

Chapelle British Cemetery, Holnon, designed by Charles Holden.

A Duhallow Block, a special memorial stone erected by the CWGC, is used when graves in designated cemeteries were either destroyed later during the war or could not be found when the cemetery was cleared. The name derives from Duhallow ADS Cemetery, Ypres, where these first special memorials were placed. Headstone and Duhallow Block, Chapelle British Cemetery, Holnon.

Wall and entrance of Grand Seraucourt British Cemetery. The powerful composition of rectangular volumes is typical of the work of Holden.

Grand Seraucourt British Cemetery. The cemetery was constructed between 1920 and 1926 and burials from many preliminary burial sites across the region were relocated here.

The town of Chauny, dating back to early medieval times, is located on the River Oise. Captured by the Germans in summer 1914, attempts to take the town during the Battle of the Marne failed. There are silent witnesses to the combat in the form of the monument to the victims of the war, by Albert Parenty and Emile Pinchon, in the centre of town, and the three military cemeteries. The German cemetery was established in autumn 1914 and contains over 1,500 burials. After the war the French Nécropole Nationale burial grounds at Chauny were created, including an ossuary, for the casualties of the Battles of the Aisne. The British cemetery extension was also created after the Armistice for the casualties of the Aisne battles. Over 1,000 bodies were relocated to the Chauny Communal Cemetery Extension.

A turning point in the First World War came with the first Battle of the Marne, in early September 1914, which resulted in a victory for the British and French troops. This had ended the rapid advances of the German army and ended the Schlieffen Plan to surprise France and capture Paris. Allied forces were able to push back the invaders. This British-French victory was followed by the first Battle of the Aisne. During the Battle of the Aisne in 1914, the town of Vailly-sur-Aisne found itself between the French and Germans, who had taken the strategic slopes of the Chemin des Dames. In 1917 an offensive to break the German defence line at the Chemin des Dames ridge was initiated. The ridge would finally be recaptured by the French in September 1918. The French Nécropole Nationale is located on the D925 Route de Soissons, not far from the River Aisne. It was first established in 1917, next to the French military aid station, and extended from 1922 onwards. There are over 1,500 burials in the grounds, mostly relocated from preliminary burial sites in the region. Next to the French cemetery is the Vailly British Cemetery, containing the remains of 674 casualties who mostly fell during the Battle of the Aisne in 1914. A simple neoclassical gate in one corner of the grounds provides entrance and is directed towards the side of the Stone of remembrance. The cemetery was designed by Sir Edwin Lutyens with Noel Rew as the assistant architect.

The ancient city of Soissons on the River Aisne was taken by the Germans in late August 1914 but would be recaptured by the French on 12 September 1914 during the Battle of the Marne. Located near the front line, the city was heavily bombarded, damaging the medieval cathedral, and was later awarded the honorary title Martyr City. Located in the square behind the cathedral is the French monument dedicated to the reconstruction, erected in 1925 and made by the twins Jan and Joël Martel. In the near vicinity, and at the culmination of the street towards the River Aisne, is the Soissons Memorial to the Missing. It was initiated by the municipality of Soissons, in cooperation with the Imperial War Graves Commission, to honour the British contribution during the First World War. The memorial commemorates 4,000 British officers and men who gave their lives in the Battles of the Aisne and the Battles of the Marne and have no known grave. It was designed by Gordon Holt and Verner Rees; the sculpture is by Eric Kennington.

On the D6 road from Soissons to Noyon is the town of Blérancourt. To commemorate the victims of the war, a monument was erected. The area between Soissons and Noyon was the site of several military encounters. After the Battle of the Marne the Germans repositioned and created a new front; French troops took control of the region in spring 1917 after the Germans had retreated to the Hindenburg Line. The bloodiest combats took place during the Spring Offensive of 1918. West of the village of Nampcel on the D335 is the Nampcel German military cemetery. After the Second World War the burial grounds were landscaped by the Volksbund Deutsche Kriegsgräberfursorge (German War Graves Committee). The present appearance was the result of a redesign of 1973, when the preliminary wooden crosses were replaced. There are over 11,000 casualties

Gate building of the Vailly British Cemetery extension, designed by Sir Edwin Lutyens, Vailly-sur-Aisne.

German military cemetery, Nampcel. Over 11,000 casualties of the First World War are buried in the grounds of Nampcel. The grounds were redesigned in 1973.

Dedication plate, Nampcel German Military Cemetery.

commemorated at the cemetery. The German military cemetery was first established in 1919 by the French as a combined Franco-German burial site; the French bodies, however, were relocated in 1922 to the Nécropole Nationale of Tracy-le-Mont. Tracy-le-Mont cemetery was created in 1920 and contains over 3,000 French casualties of the Battles of the Oise. A memorial dedicated to the war victims is located in the centre of the village, close to the church. It has the shape of an obelisk and was made by Edouard Rombaux-Roland. Tracy-le-Mont is on the precincts of the vast forests of Compiègne. On the D546 to Compiègne, close to the River Aisne, is the 11 November 1918 Memorial to the Soldiers of France, honouring the troops as defenders of their country and liberators of Alsace and Lorraine.

On 11 November 1918 the Armistice was signed, ending a war that has become known as the Great War.

Savy British Cemetery, near Saint-Quentin, was established in 1919. Burials from seven preliminary graveyards in the region were relocated to this cemetery designed by Charles Holden.

CONCLUSION

Entrance in Wrenaissance style at Ramicourt British Cemetery near Saint-Quentin, France.

Landrecies British Cemetery, Nord, France. The cemetery contains 165 burials, of which fourteen remain unidentified.

The four years of the war forever changed the world. New strategies and modern equipment had resulted in mass deaths on a scale never seen before. The need to commemorate the many fallen of the war by tangible tributes resulted in the creation of numerous memorials. These could be monuments to honour those who gave their lives, built in prominent places back home, from the village square to the middle of Whitehall, in Westminster. Monuments of grief and objects of observations, these are representations without a physical connection to the dead. Buried in preliminary graveyards first, it was decided to not return the bodies and remains of the dead to their homes. Instead, they were reinterred in carefully designed cemeteries near the battlegrounds in Flanders and northern France. For these cemeteries special memorials were ordered by the Imperial War Graves Commission: the Cross of Sacrifice, designed by Sir Reginald Blomfield, and the Stone of Remembrance, designed by Sir Edwin Lutyens. The War Stone should be understood as a stand-in tomb for the fallen. Many soldiers remained missing. The numerous names on the walls of Menin Gate are the impassive recollection of the Ypres Salient. Monuments were designed to honour these men and to give a physical place for relatives to express their sorrow. Most of these memorials were designed as part of the burial site, as one dignified composition. The first monuments to honour the fallen were created in the period that would become known as the Interwar Years. Some of them were the result of competitions such as the Canadian National Memorial in Vimy, France, while others were assignments. Eminent architects of the period were commissioned to design these commemorative monuments of grief and war cemeteries, such as Sir Edwin Lutyens, Sir Herbert Baker and Charles Holden.

By retaining the burials close to the locations where the soldiers had lost their lives, these cemeteries have become more than burial sites; they have become a tangible part of the Western Front. Memorials to the missing were intended to be monuments of grief substituting for graves. Monuments such as Menin Gate in Ypres have become meaningful expressions of grief and are part of a living memory. The names of the missing engraved on the walls are a powerful evocation, although it is the ritual of the Last Post ceremony performed daily in the Memorial Hall which makes this memorial meaningful to all. The significance of the memorial is beyond the eminence of architecture. Understanding the memorial in a much broader sense, it is a place of remembrance. It is a place of memories and a site of shared mourning. Before the decisions were made to erect memorials, the trenches of the Western Front were attracting the first visitors. Pilgrimages were undertaken to see where the martyrs had lost their lives. Visiting the mutilated landscape, still showing the scars four years of war had left behind, provides a physical connection to the suffering that is impossible to surpass. Today, the Newfoundland Memorial

Park in Beaumont-Hamel, with remnants of trenches and a countryside defaced by shelling, is one of the most visited places of the Somme region. Here the sense of place is felt, connecting the modern visitor to the front. Visiting such a place is a pilgrimage towards the Cross of Sacrifice. The memorials of the Western Front mark a countryside that is forever transformed into a landscape of remembrance. However impressive commemorative architecture can be, the victims are more than names on a wall. They are humans, as the war poets teach us when reading their poems, persons who are best honoured by not forgetting.

Tyne Cot Commonwealth War Graves Cemetery and Memorial to the Missing, containing 11,965 burials, of which 8,369 remain unidentified, making Tyne Cot the largest Commonwealth War Graves Cemetery in the world.

SELECTED BIBLIOGRAPHY

Above:
Godewaersvelde
British
Cemetery, on the
Franco-Flemish
border between
Poperinge and
Hazebrouck.

Right: Observation
post, Westhoek
Ridge, Flanders.

Ashley, Peter, *Lest We Forget: War Memorials* (English Heritage, 2004).

Barnes, Richard, *The Obelisk: A Monumental Feature in Britain* (Frontier Publishing, 2004).

Boorman, Derek, *A Century of Remembrance: One Hundred Outstanding British War Memorials* (Pen & Sword Books Ltd, 2005).

Curl, James Stevens, *A Celebration of Death: An Introduction to Some of the Buildings, Monuments, and Settings of Funerary Architecture in the Western European Tradition* (Revised ed.) (Batsford, 1980).

Geurst, Jeroen, *Cemeteries of the Great War by Sir Edwin Lutyens* (010 Publishers, 2009).

Inglis, Kenneth Stanley and Jan Brazier, *Sacred Places: War Memorials in the Australian Landscape* (3rd ed.) (Melbourne University Press, 2008).

Jacobs, M., *Zij, die vielen als helden* (Uitgave Provincie West-Vlaanderen, 1996).

Koshar, Rudy, *From Monuments to Traces: Artifacts of German Memory, 1870–1990* (University of California Press, 2000).

Low, Polly, Graham Oliver and P. J. Rhodes, *Cultures of Commemoration: War Memorials, Ancient and Modern* (British Academy Scholarship, 2012).

Moriarty, Catherine, *Sites of Memory: War Memorials at the End of the Twentieth Century* (Imperial War Museum, 1997).

Service, Alastair, *Edwardian Architecture: A Handbook to Building Design in Britain, 1890–1914* (Oxford University Press, 1977).

Skelton, Tim and Gerald Gliddon, *Lutyens and the Great War* (Frances Lincoln, 2008).

Stamp, Gavin, *The Memorial to the Missing of the Somme* (Profile Books, 2006).

Summers, Julie, *Remembered: The History of the Commonwealth War Graves Commission* (Merrell, 2007).

Winter, Jay, *Sites of Memory, Sites of Mourning: The Great War in European Cultural History* (Cambridge University Press, 1995).

Winter, Jay and Emmanuel Sivan (Eds), *War and Remembrance in the Twentieth Century* (Cambridge University Press, 1999).

ABOUT THE AUTHOR

Marcus van der Meulen studied Architecture and Interior Architecture at Leuven University and has a degree in Monument Preservation from the Institute for Conservation & Restoration in Ghent, Belgium. At Cambridge University he took courses in Architectural History including courses on classical architecture in Britain. Marcus researches the reactivation of built heritage as a preservation strategy and has published several articles about architectural history in academic journals. Marcus van der Meulen is a member of the Ghirardacci Centre of Studies, Bologna, the Association of Heritage Studies and the FRH Communication and Network Committees.

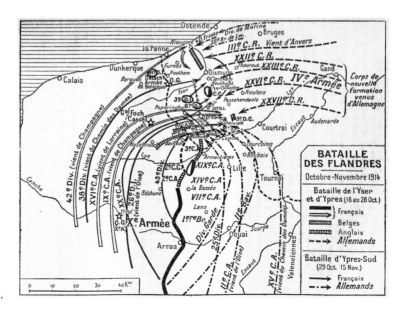

Map of the
Battle of
Flanders, 1914.

Menin Gate Memorial to the
Missing of the Ypres Salient.

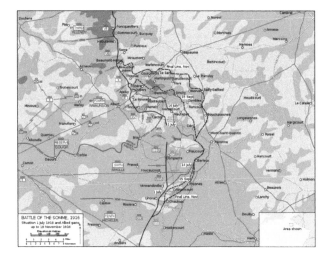